Weapons of Patton's Armies

Michael and Gladys Green

Dedication

To our good friend Fred Pernell for all his help and support during the completion of this book and many others.

First published in 2000 by MBI Publishing Company, 729 Prospect Avenue, PO Box 1, Osceola, WI 54020-0001 USA

© Michael and Gladys Green, 2000

All rights reserved. With the exception of quoting brief passages for the purposes of review, no part of this publication may be reproduced without prior written permission from the Publisher.

The information in this book is true and complete to the best of our knowledge. All recommendations are made without any guarantee on the part of the author or Publisher, who also disclaim any liability incurred in connection with the use of this data or specific details.

We recognize that some words, model names and designations, for example, mentioned herein are the property of the trademark holder. We use them for identification purposes only. This is not an official publication.

MBI Publishing Company books are also available at discounts in bulk quantity for industrial or sales-promotional use. For details write to Special Sales Manager at Motorbooks International Wholesalers & Distributors, 729 Prospect Avenue, PO Box 1, Osceola, WI 54020-0001 USA.

Library of Congress Cataloging-in-Publication Data
Green, Michael.
　Weapons of Patton's armies / by Michael and Gladys Green.
　　p. cm.
　Includes index.
　ISBN 0-7603-0821-7 (pbk. : alk. paper)
　1. United States. Army. Army, 3rd—Equipment. 2. World War, 1939–1945—Equipment and supplies. 3. United States. Army—Weapons systems—History—20th century. I. Green, Gladys. II. Title.

D769.26 3rd.G7424　2000
940.54'1'028—dc21　　　　　00-033260

Edited by Mike Haenggi

Designed by Terry Webster

Printed in the United States of America

Contents

Acknowledgments 4

Introduction 5

Chapter 1
Infantry Weapons 6

Chapter 2
Artillery Weapons 40

Chapter 3
Armored Fighting Vehicles 72

Chapter 4
Antitank Weapons 103

Chapter 5
Antiaircraft Weapons 130

Appendix 158

Index 159

Acknowledgments

Special thanks are due to the National Archives, Patton Museum of Cavalry and Armor, Virginia Museum of Military Vehicles, Inc., the British Army Tank Museum, and the George S. Patton Jr. Historical Society, all of whose support and help made this book possible. Thanks are also due to the U.S. Army Armor School Library at Fort Knox, Kentucky, and the Fourth and Fifth Armored Division Associations. George Hoffman of the Sixth Armored Division Association was kind enough to allow use of pictures from his division's files. Individuals who made an extra effort in helping include Charles Lemons, Patton Museum curator; Judy Stephenson, Armor School librarian; David Fletcher, British Army Tank Museum Curator; Allan Cors, director of the Virginia Museum of Military Vehicles; and Charles Province, president and founder of the Patton Historical Society. Other friends who offered their kind assistance include Jacques Littlefield, Dean and Nancy Kleffman, John P. Wallace, Frank Buck, Dennis Riva, Milton Halsey Jr., Dick Hunnicutt, Frank Schulz, Andreas Kirchhoff, Richard Byrd, Richard Cox, George Bradford, Mert Wreford, Richard Pemberton, and Karl and Carol Vonder Linden.

Note to the reader:
A visit to the world-famous Patton Museum of Cavalry and Armor, at Fort Knox, Kentucky, allows the viewing of various Patton artifacts as well the weapons and equipment employed by both the U.S. Army and the Germans during World War II. Information on museum hours of operation and how to visit the museum can be obtained by writing to Building 4554, Fort Knox, Kentucky 40121-0208. The museum's web site is at http://147.238.100.101/museum/

A valuable source of information on Patton the man is the George S. Patton Jr. Historical Society. The society publishes a semiannual newsletter devoted to the study of the man. The society can be reached by writing to 3116 Thorn Street, San Diego, California 92104-4618. The society's web site is at: http://hometown.aol.com/PattonGHQ/homeghq.html

Introduction

Between the start of America's military participation in World War I and the end of World War II, the U.S. Army selected, tested, and eventually placed into production a wide variety of weapons ranging from .30-caliber rifles to massive 240-mm artillery pieces. This book is a general overview of many of the weapons used by the soldiers who served under the command of George S. Patton between 1918 and 1945.

This book is not intended as a definitive technical history of the weapons selected by the authors for review. Size and format restrictions imposed by the publisher make that impossible. Rather, the authors have concentrated on the rationale behind the selection of the weapons by the army. We have included some of Patton's views on the combat use of certain weapons to add insight into his thinking.

Due to the very technical nature of some of the weapons and their employment described in this book, the authors have decided to include a number of sidebars within the text to better acquaint the reader with unfamiliar terms and concepts. Readers who wish to seek more detailed information on the weapons reviewed in this work will find a small listing of the hundreds of excellent reference works in the suggested reading list.

Chapter One

INFANTRY WEAPONS

The most primitive killing weapon in the hands of Patton's soldiers from World War I through World War II was the bayonet. While millions of men carried the weapon into various theaters of war, only a miniscule number actually used it in combat. However, no man could be sure that he would never need to fight with it.

The U.S. Army believed very strongly that all soldiers armed with a bayonet had to master its use. It believed that if a man did not have confidence in his ability with the bayonet, he had a weakness in his fighting skills and was less of a soldier.

Patton would sum up his feelings regarding the use of the bayonet in combat in a letter of instruction to the senior commanders of the Third Army, dated April 3, 1944:

"Few men are killed by the bayonet; many are scared of it. Bayonets should be fixed when the fire fight starts. Bayonets must be sharpened by the individual soldier. The German hates the bayonet and is inferior to our men with it. Our men should know this."

Prior to World War II (1939–1945) the army's standard rifle bayonet was the M1905, adopted into service at the beginning of the twentieth century. It had a blade 16 inches long and was equipped with wooden grips. The Ordnance Department's Rock Island Arsenal and Springfield Armory built large numbers for use by the army in World War I (1914–1918). During the 1920s and 1930s the existing supply of M1905 bayonets was more than enough to meet the needs of the small peacetime American army.

As the army began to grow in size in the months before the Japanese sneak attack on Pearl Harbor (December 7, 1941) the

His face covered with a gas mask, an American soldier stands guard with his rifle and attached M1905 bayonet. In 1943 the army, with input from the Marine Corps, came up with a revised bayonet training manual to improve the skills of its soldiers in up-close combat engagements. The revised manual, while broadly similar to an older World War I manual, was considerably altered in a number of important respects. The biggest change was a greater importance on more realistic training exercises. *National Archives*

6 **Infantry Weapons**

Ordnance Department anticipated a need for more bayonets. Since the Rock Island Arsenal and the Springfield Armory were busy with other projects, the Ordnance Department arranged with a number of civilian companies to resume production of the M1905 bayonet. Due to a number of manufacturing problems and shortages of raw materials, the various civilian firms awarded contracts to build the bayonet could not undertake full-scale production until September 1942. By the summer of 1943 they were up to speed and providing the army with more than 200,000 M1905 bayonets a month.

To speed up production and lower the cost of the M1905 bayonet a number of manufacturing shortcuts were taken during World War II. The

A young U.S. Army soldier poses for the photographer with his rifle and M1905 bayonet in the ready position. In 1943 the Army introduced a new type of bayonet training course. Before, a soldier would attack a sequence of identical dummies arrayed in a line on a parade field setting. The soldier was now required to complete a bayonet assault course from 200 to 300 yards long and including as many man-made and local terrain obstacles as possible. National Archives

U.S. Army soldiers are seen practicing their skills on a pre-1943 bayonet training course. In the new simplified 1943 bayonet training manual the Army did away with a number of superfluous bayonet movements and formations taught in the older World War I manual. In their place the Army incorporated group assault tactics developed by the Marine Corps, which stressed teamwork when assaulting an enemy position with the bayonet. National Archives

Chapter One 7

In an artfully composed photograph, two lines of U.S. Army soldiers face each other at the ready with their rifles and M1 bayonets. A World War II army manual stated: "The bayonet is an offensive weapon. With it, aggressiveness wins. Hesitation, preliminary maneuvering, and fencing are fatal. The delay of a fraction of a second may mean death. The bayonet fighter attacks in a fast, relentless assault until his opponent is destroyed." *National Archives*

Pictured in the hands of a U.S. Army soldier during World War II is a Caliber .45 Automatic Pistol M1911A1. The weapon is magazine-fed, recoil-operated, and self-loading. The gas pressure generated when the cartridge is fired forces the recoiling parts to the rear. During recoil the empty cartridge case is ejected, the recoil spring is compressed, and the hammer cocked. When the recoil movement is completed, the compressed recoil spring expands, forcing the recoiling parts forward into the battery, chambering a round of ammunition and placing the pistol in the ready-to-fire position again. *National Archives*

only visible change between the older and newer versions of the M1905 bayonet was the use of plastic grips and a parkerized blade. Over one million M1905 bayonets were assembled during World War II. It was the standard issue bayonet for the army's rifles.

New and Rebuilt Bayonets

With the ever-increasing number of wheeled and tracked vehicles entering army service in the early part of World War II, it soon became apparent that the impressive 16-inch knife blade of the M1905 bayonet was impractical when soldiers were being transported in tight confines. In late 1942, the Cavalry Board requested that a shorter version of the M1905 bayonet be adopted. A number of M1905 bayonets had 6 inches of their tips removed. The First Cavalry Division subjected the modified bayonets to field tests. The

8 Infantry Weapons

tests showed the modification to be a success, and with the support of the Infantry Board, the shortened bayonet was standardized into service as the Bayonet M1 in February 1943. Production of the bayonet began in April 1943 and continued until August 1945, with over two million units delivered to the army. It would be the most common bayonet in army service in World War II.

Not wanting to discard the large number of original long-bladed M1905 bayonets, the Ordnance Department contracted with several civilian firms to modify the older bayonets by grinding 6 inches from the blade and then giving them new tips. Over a million M1905 bayonets were converted into the shorter M1 pattern in this manner.

When the army's semiautomatic carbine was placed into service in late 1941, it had no provision for mounting a bayonet. Demand by the units in the field forced the Ordnance Department to come up with something quickly. It was decided to employ a modified M3 trench knife in the role. In its new configuration, the weapon was designated the M4 bayonet-knife. It was standardized in April 1944. Over two million were produced between July 1944 and August 1945.

Handguns

The most widely used handgun in U.S. Army service during World War II was named in typical government fashion and called the Pistol, Automatic, Caliber Model M1911A1. The need for the gun began in the early 1900s. During the uprising of the Moro tribes in the Philippines, it was found that the fanatic tribesmen were not being stopped when hit by rounds from the .38-caliber revolvers then in use by American troops. This lack of stopping power was one of the factors that led to the adoption in 1911 of the original version of the .45-caliber weapon designated the Pistol, Automatic, Caliber Model 1911. Soldiers usually referred to it as the ".45" or the ".45 automatic."

The M1911 was designed and patented by John M. Browning, who was a renowned inventor of lever-action rifles and automatic pistols. The actual development and early production of the M1911 was by the Colt Patent Firearms Company. This resulted in the weapon also being called the "Colt .45" or just the "Colt." During World War I Colt could not keep up with the demand for the weapon, so production was also undertaken by the Springfield Armory.

Coming out of the bottom escape hatch of a U.S. Army Sherman medium tank is a tanker crewman armed with a Caliber .45 Automatic Pistol M1911A1. Many American tankers in World War II did not favor wearing the M1911A1 in its holster because it could catch on objects when leaving their vehicle quickly. The magazine on the weapon holds seven rounds when fully loaded. Empty, the pistol weighs approximately 2 1/2 pounds. *National Archives*

Chapter One 9

The U.S. Army Ordnance Department

The one segment of the U.S. Army most directly concerned with weapon development was the Ordnance Department. It was responsible for the design, procurement, distribution, and maintenance of all the army's ordnance (weapons). The first mention of the Ordnance Department appeared in a resolution of the Continental Congress in 1778 concerning the assignment of certain artillery officers the responsibility for the issue of ordnance supplies to the troops in the field.

During World War II the Ordnance Department issued some 1,860 different models of major pieces of fighting equipment; of these about 1,200 were models of new or improved design. In mid-1940 the Ordnance Department consisted of 334 officers and 3,950 enlisted men. When American troops went ashore in Normandy on D-Day, June 6, 1944, the Ordnance Department had grown to nearly 24,000 officers and over 325,000 enlisted personnel.

Before March 1942, it was the job of the army's individual combat arms, such as the infantry or cavalry, to work with the Ordnance Department in determining the characteristics needed in any given weapon or accessory to fulfill a definite military purpose. After March 1942, the newly formed Army Ground Forces (AGF) took over the responsibility for informing the Ordnance Department what weapons the different combat branches needed.

When the Ordnance Department and the Army Ground Forces agreed upon the principal military characteristics of a new weapon, the Ordnance Department worked out a design, built a pilot model, and subjected it to tests.

The using branches then studied its performance, suggested modifications, and scrutinized the resulting modified weapon. If it appeared to be acceptable to the using branch, the Ordnance Department made a small number for tests under conditions similar to their intended combat employment. It was the job of the using branches to conduct service tests. When the using branch and the Ordnance Department agreed that the weapon was satisfactory. The army's General Staff authorized the Ordnance Department to accept, or "standardize" the weapon and order it into full-scale production.

The Ordnance Department had planned on contracting with a number of civilian firms to build the M1911, but the war ended before full-scale production was undertaken by outside contractors.

Based on some minor design problems uncovered during its use in World War I, the M1911 was redesigned after the conflict. The modified version was designated the Pistol, Automatic, Caliber Model M1911A1 in 1926. Very few of these new pistols were built prior to World War II because of the large existing inventory of M1911 models from World War I.

With America's entry into World War II, Colt quickly began full-scale production of the M1911A1. Because Colt could not produce enough automatic pistols to meet all the army's needs, the Ordnance Department contracted with four civilian firms to produce M1911A1 pistols. Roughly two million M1911A1 pistols were produced during the war years. Despite this impressive number of M1911A1 pistols built, they were often scarce during World War II.

A comparison between the M1911A1 and various types of German semiautomatic pistols comes from a U.S. Army report published in March 1945:

"The standard caliber .45 U.S. automatic is preferred to any of the German-issue pistols. The greater striking power is desired over the advantage of a lightweight weapon. The safety features are considered superior to those of German pistols."

The operation of the M1911 and M1911A1 pistols was identical, with both weapons being recoil-operated. Like all military handguns, they were characterized by their relatively short range and small magazine capacity, due to their purpose—which is generally defensive. Effective range in well-trained hands could be up to 100 yards. For the less qualified majority, the effective range could drop to 15 yards or less. During World War II, the army sought to restrict issue of the M1911A1 pistol to officers, troops manning crew-served weapons, and rear area service troops.

While the M1911 and the M1911A1 pistols were called automatic weapons, this term was inaccurate. A fully automatic weapon keeps firing as long as the trigger is held back. A semiautomatic weapon unlocks, extracts, ejects, cocks, and reloads automatically, however the trigger must be pulled each time to fire a round. The .45-caliber automatic pistol was a semiautomatic weapon by definition, since each shot required a trigger pull.

The only other handgun to see service in any type of numbers (300,000) with the army in World War II was the .45-caliber Model 1917 double-action revolver. The revolver was a leftover from World War I and had been built by both Smith & Wesson and Colt. About 15,000 of these weapons were refurbished for army use in 1941.

In Western Europe during World War II a U.S. Army soldier takes the time to clean the barrel of his Rifle, Caliber .30 M1903A3. Notice the chalked-on statement on the tent behind the infantryman, no doubt added for the benefit of the photographer to make the picture more interesting. The M1903A3 and its production predecessor, the M1903 (Modified), can be distinguished from the original version of the rifle by simplified stocks. *National Archives*

U.S. Army infantrymen are seen training sometime in the 1920s with the Rifle, Caliber .30, M1903. Most soldiers simply called it the "Springfield." The weapon was originally adopted at the beginning of the twentieth century as a replacement for the troublesome .30-40 Krag-Jorgensen rifle, the Army's first magazine-fed rifle. The Springfield weighed a little over eight pounds and had an overall length of 43.5 inches. *National Archives*

The primary users of the .45-caliber Model 1917 revolver in World War II were rear area support personnel, although some were used by front line troops. During the fighting in North Africa (1942-1943) many American soldiers preferred the revolver over the .45-caliber M1911A1 automatic pistol, since it was less prone to jamming in the dusty conditions prevalent in that area of operations.

Bolt-Action Rifles

The preferred infantry weapon of the U.S. Army in World War I was the Rifle, Caliber .30, Model of 1903. Most soldiers simply referred to as the "Springfield," since it was designed, developed, and largely manufactured at the Springfield Arsenal. During World War I the Ordnance Department also undertook production of the weapon at the Rock Island Arsenal.

The Springfield was a bolt-action rifle, weighing a little over eight pounds, with a five-round internal box magazine. It fired the powerful long-range M1906 .30-caliber cartridge better known as the .30-06. This round would go on to become the standard rifle and machine gun cartridge for the U.S. Army until the 1960s.

In 1936 the army decided to replace the Springfield with a new semiautomatic rifle. Due to numerous delays in fielding the new weapon, the Springfield would remain in widespread army service for the first couple of years of World War II. Many of Patton's troops were equipped with Springfield rifles during the fighting in North Africa and Sicily (November 1942 through July 1943). Some Springfield rifles would remain in army service until the very end of the war.

The desperate need for rifles by the army during the opening stages of World War II forced the Ordnance Department to resume production of the Springfield rifle. Since the Springfield Armory and the Rock Island Arsenal were already busy with other projects, the Ordnance Department contracted with the Remington Arms Company to resume production.

Due to a combination of worn out tooling equipment and inexperienced workers, the production of new Springfield rifles by Remington remained low at first. The Ordnance Department, working with the company, decided to simplify the weapon's construction to increase the production output. The revised weapon was designated the Rifle, Caliber .30, M1903 (Modified). Not long afterward, Remington engineers

Chapter One   11

An American soldier in World War II takes aim with the sniper version of the M1903A3 rifle. The official designation of the weapon was Rifle, Caliber .30, M1903A4 (Sniper's). Other than the removal of the standard front and rear sights and their replacement with a commercially available scope, no special efforts were made by the builder to produce a weapon more accurate than the standard M1903 rifle. This lack of concern for the exacting demands of sniping made the M1903A4 a poor second-rate contender when compared to far-superior German sniper rifles. *National Archives*

made some additional modifications to the Springfield rifle design to further speed up production. The resulting version of the Springfield was designated the Rifle, Caliber .30, Model of M1903A3.

To increase the number of M1903A3 rifles available, the Ordnance Department contracted with the L.C. Smith & Corona Typewriter Company to produce the same weapon. Both Remington and Smith-Corona would provide the army with a large number of the M1903A3 rifles until their contracts were canceled in early 1944.

The most interesting variant of the M1903A3 rifle to see service in World War II was a sniper version. The weapon was designated the Rifle, Caliber .30, M1903A4 (Sniper's). It came about due to a shortage of sniper rifles within the army in the early days of World War II.

To put a sniper rifle into service as quickly as possible, the Ordnance Department allowed Remington to use commercially made scopes on the weapon. The scopes proved unable to stand up to the rigors of combat and proved somewhat

An American soldier takes aim with his World War I vintage Browning Automatic Rifle, Model of 1918, during a 1920s training exercise. The weapon was better known to most soldiers simply as the "BAR." From 1918 until 1957, except for a few brief exceptions, every rifle squad in the U.S. Army was authorized a single BAR. During World War II it was not uncommon to find American infantry squads equipped with more than one BAR. *National Archives*

of a disappointment in service. Despite its shortcomings, Remington would build almost 30,000 examples of the M1903A4 sniper rifle during the war years.

During World War I, American factories under contract with the British government manufactured a bolt-action rifle known as the Pattern 1914. It fired the British .303 cartridge. When the British contracts were completed, the Ordnance Department asked the various companies to build a version of the same rifle chambered to fire the standard American .30-06 caliber service cartridge. The modified British weapon in American service was designated the Rifle, Caliber .30, Model of 1917. Most American soldiers just called it the "Enfield." Over two million were built between 1917 and 1919. More Enfields were in service with American troops in World War I than the American-designed and built Springfield.

After World War I the entire inventory of Enfields was consigned to reserve storage, as the army decided to standardize on the Springfield rifle. As war clouds loomed over the United States in 1940 and 1941, the Enfields were brought out of storage and refurbished. Many were sent to England in mid-1940 as part of a lend-lease pro-

Pictured in the early 1940s during a training exercise are two U.S. Army soldiers armed with the Rifle, Caliber .30, Model of 1917, commonly called the "Enfield." The soldiers are clothed in experimental camouflaged uniforms. The Enfield weighed 8.18 pounds and had a length of 46.3 inches. The ungainly looking Enfield was never as popular in service with American troops as the better balanced and more streamlined Springfield. *National Archives*

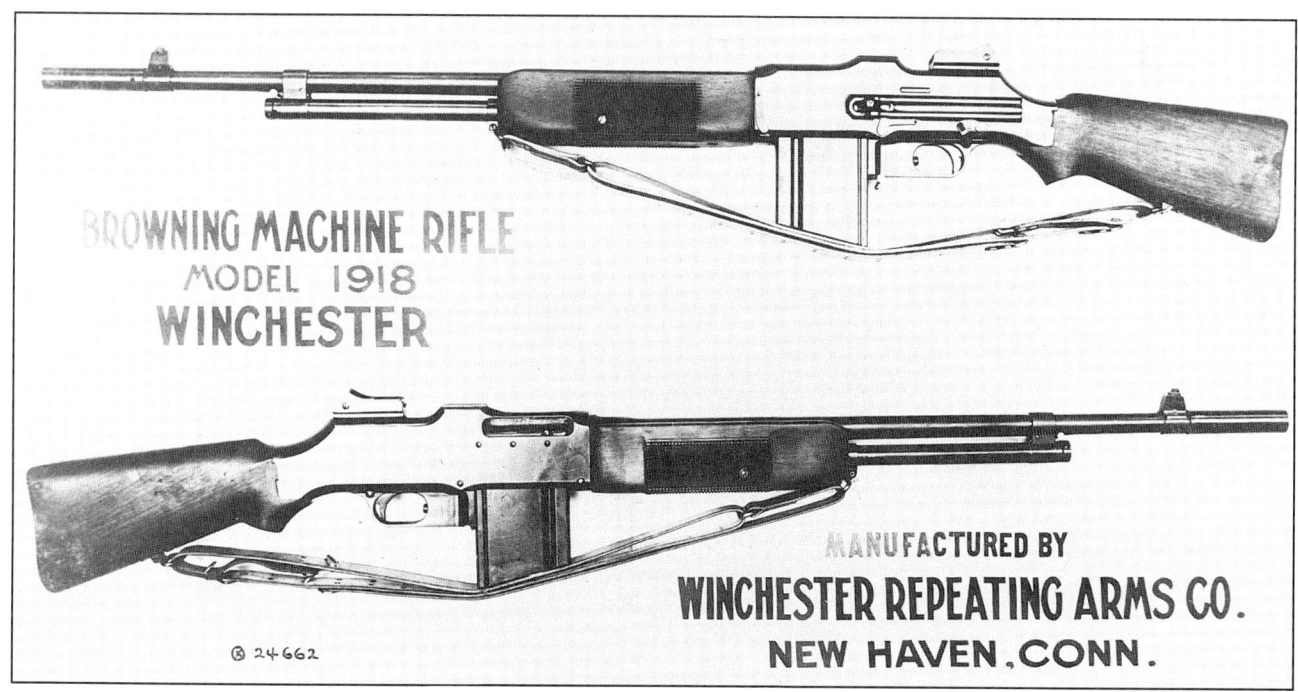

In gas-operated weapons like the BAR, a portion of the expanding gases behind the bullet is tapped off into a gas cylinder located beneath the barrel. The hole connecting the barrel and cylinder is always near the muzzle end of a gas-operated weapon. As the bullet passes this hole, gasses enter the cylinder, strike a piston, and push this piston rearward. The piston is connected by a rod to an operating mechanism of the weapon, such as the bolt. The piston carries the bolt rearward with it, unlocking, extracting, ejecting, and cocking the weapon. *National Archives*

Chapter One 13

The BAR could fire either ball or armor-piercing (AP) ammunition at a muzzle velocity of 2,800 feet per second. The maximum range on the weapon was 3,500 yards. The two pre-1940 versions of the BAR could fire in semiautomatic or in full automatic mode. During World War I and II the semiautomatic firing feature was rarely used since troops preferred firing short two- or three-round automatic bursts, rather than fumble in the heat of combat for the selector switch. *National Archives*

The final production version of the BAR was designated the M1918A2 and can be seen in the hands of the American soldier in the foreground of the picture. The key spotting feature to distinguish the M1918A2 version of the BAR from the earlier models was the cut-down wooden forend. This was done to expose more of the metal surface of the barrel for cooling purposes and prevent charring of the wood during sustained firing. *National Archives*

gram to strengthen the hard-pressed British forces. A number of Enfields also were issued to army units in the United States for training purposes. Some were even sent overseas with Patton's forces during the invasion of North Africa in November 1942. No new production of Enfields was undertaken during World War II.

Automatic Rifles

Another World War I era army weapon that saw extensive service in World War II was the Browning Automatic Rifle, commonly called the "BAR" by American soldiers in both conflicts. The BAR was a gas-operated weapon, with a 20-round detachable box magazine, weighing a bit over 16 pounds in its original form. It fired the army's standard .30-06-caliber service cartridge. In the field the BAR performed the role of light machine gun within the army infantry squads.

John M. Browning first conceived the weapon at the beginning of the twentieth century. Due to lack of army interest at the time, he did not pursue its development. It was not until May 1917, one month after the United States entered World War I, that the army solicited various gun designers to submit designs to fulfill the requirement for an automatic rifle. Browning renewed work on his earlier automatic rifle design and provided to the Ordnance Department a hand-tooled prototype. The prototype weapon from Browning outshone all its competitors in the firing tests and was quickly ordered into full-scale production in 1917 as the Browning Machine Rifle, Model 1918. The Ordnance Department did not call it the Model 1917 to prevent possible confusion arising from the existence of the Browning Model 1917 Machine Gun.

Winchester Repeating Arms Company and the Marlin-Rockwell Corporation built over 100,000 units of the M1918. After World War I the Ordnance Department came up with two modified versions of the original BAR. The first appeared in the early 1920s and was intended for use by the army's horsed cavalry units. It was designated the Caliber .30 Browning Machine Rifle M1922, and featured a bipod, a new finned barrel, and the provision for full automatic fire only. Only 470 examples were completed.

Another limited production version of the BAR appeared in 1937. It was designated the Caliber .30 Browning Automatic Rifle M1918A1 and featured an improved gas system, plus a hinged butt plate at the rear of the stock. Like the original version of the BAR, it retained the ability to be fired either semiautomatic or full automatic.

When America's entry into World War II became just a matter of time, the Ordnance Department authorized the final production version of the BAR, designated the M1918A2. It featured a number of changes to the basic BAR design, including the deletion of the semiautomatic firing feature. The M1918A2 could only be fired in the full-automatic mode, although the rate of fire could be adjusted to 350 or 500 rounds per minute. The need for semiautomatic fire in the last version of the BAR was eliminated, due to the introduction of a new semiautomatic rifle in 1937.

The first production examples of the M1918A2 were based on the conversion of exist-

The M1 seen here on the shoulder of an American soldier was considered by most military men as the best infantry rifle to come out of World War II. It was loaded by carefully inserting eight cartridges contained in a charger into the weapon's open receiver. Once correctly placed over the receiver, the charger, with the eight cartridges it contained, was pushed with the user's thumb into an internal magazine housed within the wooden stock. Each time the weapon was fired, a new cartridge automatically fed into the firing chamber. *National Archives*

Pictured lying prone in a cotton field during an early 1940s training exercise is an American soldier armed with an early model of the Rifle, Caliber .30, M1. It was better known to all as the "M1." The 9.5-pound weapon fired either ball or armor-piercing (AP) ammunition at a muzzle velocity of 2,800 feet per second. The maximum effective range of the 43.6-inch semiautomatic M1 was 3,500 yards. *National Archives*

Chapter One 15

ing M1918 and M1918A1 weapons from army reserve stockpiles. This process would continue until the supply of weapon was exhausted. At least 25,000 early model BARs were transferred to England between 1940 and 1941 in a show of solidarity between the two countries.

After the United States entered World War II, the Ordnance Department contracted with two civilian firms to build the new models of the M1918A2. The New England Small Arms Corporation built 168,000 during the war years. International Business Machine (IBM) completed only 25,000 units of the M1918A2 before the Ordnance Department canceled its contract.

Combat use of the BAR during World War I and II established its reputation as a reliable and hard-hitting weapon that was in great demand by front-line soldiers. Due to its popularity, it was not uncommon for infantry units to acquire extra BARs to supplement their squad-level firepower.

Semiautomatic Rifles

During World War II the standard infantry weapon in the hands of U.S. Army soldiers was the Rifle, Caliber .30, M1. Most soldiers better knew it as the "M1." Patton called it "the greatest weapon ever made." The first production examples were delivered to the troops in August 1937. It was a semiautomatic, gas-operated weapon, weighing about 9 1/2 pounds. Fully loaded, the M1 held eight rounds secured in a metal clip that was loaded as a single unit into the weapon's receiver. The empty clip was ejected with the last empty cartridge case. John C. Garand, chief civilian Ordnance Department engineer at the Springfield Armory, was responsible for the design of the rifle.

The genesis of the M1 began shortly after World War, I when the Ordnance Department developed a requirement for a semiautomatic rifle. The intent was to replace the bolt-action Springfield. The Ordnance Department had actually begun looking into fielding a semiautomatic rifle in 1901 without much success. Instead, the army adopted the Springfield rifle in 1903.

The advantages of a semiautomatic rifle versus a bolt-action were clear to many in the Ordnance Department. They included greater accuracy in rapid fire due to the elimination of having to operate a bolt, a greater volume of fire per minute per man, more fire-power against low-flying enemy aircraft, and a decrease in time required in instructing new recruits in marksmanship.

U.S. Army infantrymen armed with the M1 jump to shore from a small wooden assault boat during World War II. When the last round in the Garand was fired, the empty clip located within the weapon's internal magazine was automatically ejected from the receiver and the bolt remained in its rearmost position ready for the insertion of another fully loaded clip. The need to insert only a fully loaded clip into the M1 and the inability to "top up" with a single round was seen as a design shortcoming by many weapon experts. *National Archives*

A grim-faced American soldier armed with an M1 stands over the body of a German infantryman who fell to his accurate fire. Each U.S. Army infantry squad on paper consisted of 12 soldiers, including a staff sergeant who was the squad leader, and a sergeant who was the assistant squad leader. Both men were normally armed with M1s. The remaining 10 men in the squad were armed with nine M1s and a single BAR. *National Archives*

Two American soldiers in France during World War II are pictured cleaning their disassembled M1 carbines. Within every U.S. Army rifle squad, the 10 men serving under the squad and assistant squad leader were divided into two groups. One group was known as the automatic rifle team and consisted of three men armed with one BAR and two M1s. The remaining seven men armed with M1s acted as the maneuver element of the squad. *National Archives*

Many American- and foreign-designed semiautomatic rifles were tested in the early 1920s with limited success. None could meet the Ordnance Department's stringent requirements. Foreign armies, such as the German army, also interested in adopting a semiautomatic rifle, gave up on the idea and incorporated a light machine gun into every infantry squad. There were some in the U.S. Army who also favored the use of light machineguns at the squad level. Others, who believed that light machine guns would complicate infantry squad tactics and reduce their mobility, overruled them.

The requirements mandated by the Ordnance Department for its proposed semiautomatic rifle were numerous. The weapon had to be well balanced and adapted to shoulder firing. It must also be simple, strong and compact, and adapted to ease of manufacture. The weapon must be designed so that the magazine could be fed from clips or chargers, and that no special materials, such as grease or oil, would be needed for the proper functioning of the weapon.

After the Ordnance Department conducted its first shoot-off for a semiautomatic rifle, a decision was made to replace the army's standard .30-06 service cartridge with a smaller and lighter .276-caliber cartridge. This was not the first time that the army and the Ordnance Department had flirted with smaller caliber ammunition for its service rifles. The main rationalization behind this decision was to produce a rifle weighing less than 8.5 pounds.

The Ordnance Department invited all interested contenders with semiautomatic rifles able to chamber a .276-caliber cartridge to present their designs during a second round of testing to be conducted in 1932. It was during this occasion that John Garand, who worked for the Ordnance Department, presented his candidate rifle firing a .276-caliber cartridge. It performed very well in all categories and generated much interest among all concerned.

Unfortunately for Garand, all his work on developing a reliable and accurate semiautomatic rifle firing a .276-caliber round was negated when

General Douglas MacArthur, army chief of staff, decided to stick with the standard .30-06-rifle cartridge. Garand was forced back to the drawing board. Fortunately for the U.S. Army, Garand would come up with a semiautomatic rifle firing the .30-06-caliber cartridge that met all the Ordnance Department's requirements except the weight, which had crept up to 9.5 pounds. In 1936 the army decided to overlook the increase in weight, and officially adopted the M1 as its standard infantry rifle.

Widespread introduction of the M1 into army service was delayed at first by numerous production problems at the Springfield Armory. Most of the problems were related to the lack of modern machine tools necessary to build the new fairly complex weapon. Congress decided to appropriate almost $2 million in 1938 to completely retool the Springfield Armory in an effort to speed up production of the M1. This sum supplemented the approximately $1 million that had already been spent at Springfield for new equipment and gauges in 1935 on behalf of M1 development. Even with the new machine tools, the Ordnance Department realized by 1939 that Springfield Armory could not meet future requirements.

The Ordnance Department decided that additional M1s should be obtained from private industry. When it called for bids in the summer of 1939 to build the semiautomatic rifle, both Remington and Winchester responded. Of the two companies, Winchester submitted the lower bid and won the contract. By the end of World War II the Springfield Armory and Winchester together managed to build over four million M1s.

Despite its popular wartime image as a tough and very dependable weapon, the early production models of the M1s were plagued by some minor teething problems, which the Ordnance

A young American army officer studies a map on the hood of his jeep during World War II. He keeps his 35.6-inch-long M1 carbine by his side for quick use. The carbine was originally intended only as a replacement weapon for those officers and men authorized to use pistols or submachine guns. Its popularity soon saw its use spread to front line combat troops. *National Archives*

Chapter One 19

On the top of a U.S. Army tank turret, a tanker is posing for the photographer, along with his superior officer, by aiming a Submachine Gun, Caliber .45, M1928A1 at an imaginary target. Most soldiers called the weapon the "Thompson." This production example of the Thompson pictured is equipped with a 50-round detachable drum magazine. It fired ball ammunition at a muzzle velocity of 920-feet-per-second. *National Archives*

Department considered normal in the development of a new weapon. The infantry was well aware of these problems and accepted Ordnance Department assurances that the defects could and would eventually be corrected.

Unfortunately for the Ordnance Department, these minor problems attracted the attention of the National Rifle Association (NRA) and Congress, which almost had M1 production canceled in the spring of 1940. A number of newspapers and magazine articles criticizing the M1 only added fuel to the controversy. *Life* magazine called it "one of the greatest military squabbles in U.S. history." Much of the negative publicity over the M1 could have been avoided if the Ordnance Department had taken the NRA into its confidence, instead of stonewalling the organization when legitimate questions arose over M1 performance.

The squabble over the M1 would not end until late 1940, when the Marine Corps decided to conduct a series of tests to compare it to a competing semiautomatic weapon named the Johnson, after its designer, Melvin Johnson. Also in the test was the army's standard bolt-action Springfield rifle.

The Marine Corps tests results showed the M1 to be clearly superior in almost all respects to the Johnson. The old reliable Springfield had actually led the field in accuracy, ruggedness, and

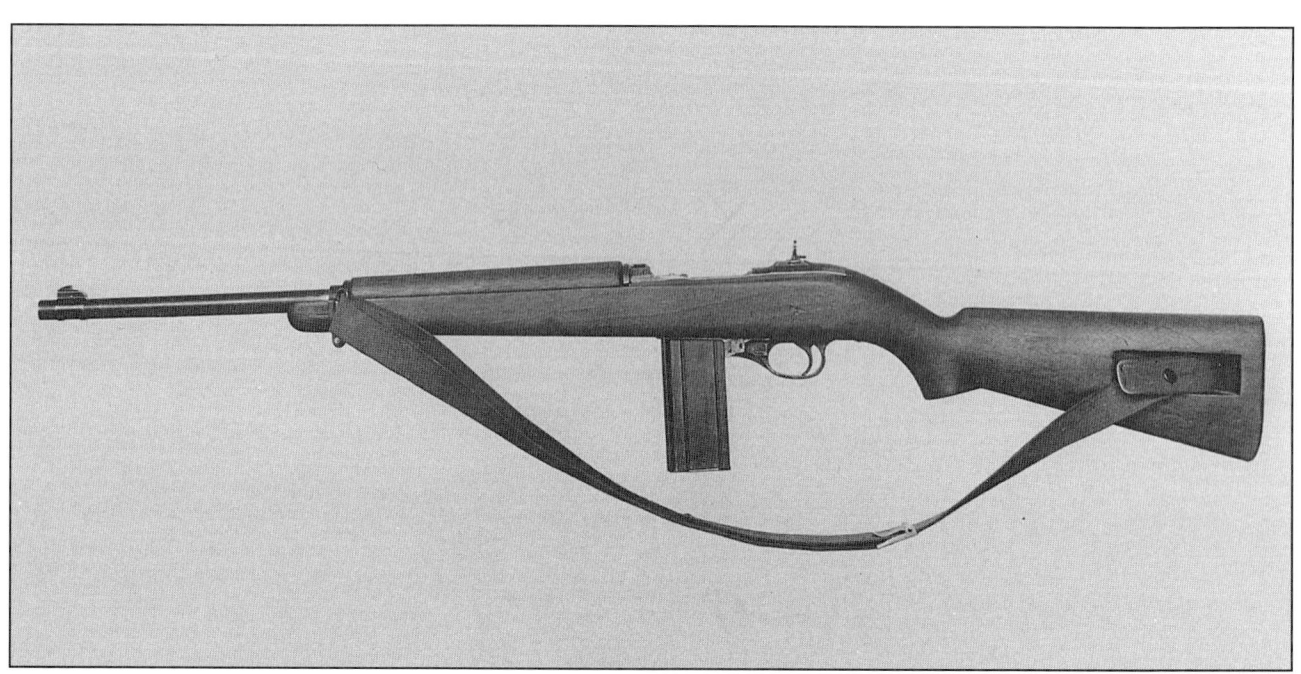

The Carbine, Caliber .30, M1, better known as just the "M1 Carbine," was a 5.2-pound gas-operated semiautomatic weapon fed by an external 15-round detachable box magazine. It would be built in greater numbers than any other American military small arms during World War II. Firing ball or armor piercing (AP), it had a muzzle velocity of 1,970 feet per second. The maximum range was 2,200 yards. *National Archives*

dependability, but it simply could not produce as much firepower as the semiautomatics rifles. The Marine Corps decided on the basis of its test to adopt the M1 into service. This decision effectively ended the public and congressional criticism of the weapon.

Carbines

After World War I the Ordnance Department began to think about the need for a new class of lightweight weapons that would fall in range and power between the standard infantry rifle and the M1911A1 pistol. Nothing came of the idea until early 1938, when the infantry branch asked the Ordnance Department to develop a .30-caliber carbine weighing five pounds or less, and accurate up to 300 yards.

The definition of a carbine is a light rifle with a short barrel. During the nineteenth century, the carbine was a traditional weapon of the cavalry, as the larger infantry rifles were unsuitable for men on horseback. By the beginning of the twentieth century, it disappeared from use within the U.S. Army when the 1903 Springfield rifle proved satisfactory for both mounted and foot troops.

The Ordnance Department initially resisted the infantry branch's request for a new carbine, as it would require a new type of intermediate-power ammunition. Eventually, ordnance dropped its objections to the project, and in the fall of 1940 set up a definite requirement for a carbine. The Winchester Company was asked by the Ordnance Department to undertake the design of a new cartridge for the proposed carbine, since it had extensive experience with ammunition for semiautomatic weapons. In November 1940 Winchester submitted for testing purposes a cartridge based on one of its existing designs. The Ordnance Department tests went very well, and the new cartridge was ordered into production in small experimental lots.

While the Ordnance Department had Winchester working on the development of ammunition for the proposed carbine, it solicited various manufacturers and designers to submit

An American infantry squad is pictured firing at enemy personnel. The soldier in the center of the picture is armed with a midproduction version of the M1928A1 Thompson. Features that made the Thompson so popular with American and Allied soldiers in World War II were its reliability in action and its knockdown power at short ranges. At longer ranges, the accuracy and killing power of the Thompson dropped a great deal, compared to the M1 semiautomatic rifle. *National Archives*

Chapter One   21

A tanker from the famous Second Armored Division poses with a midproduction M1928A1 Thompson. In place of the 50-round detachable drum magazine the weapon is equipped with a 20-round detachable box magazine. Key spotting features for the M1928A1 version of the Thompson are the small knob-like cocking handle on top of the weapon's receiver and the compensator at the muzzle end of the barrel. The compensator was designed to help keep the barrel down when firing the weapon by venting some of the gases generated during firing upward. *National Archives*

prototype weapons for test purposes by the summer of 1941. A number of candidates were tested, but none was entirely satisfactory. One result of the tests was the dropping, by the Ordnance Department, of the requirement for full-automatic fire. Instead, it was decided that the proposed carbine should fire in the semi-automatic mode only.

Since the first round of tests had not produced what the Ordnance Department was looking for, it rescheduled a new series of service tests to be completed by September 15, 1941. It urged inventors and designers who had not entered the initial round of tests to submit potential candidates. Winchester entered the second round of completion for the proposed carbine and entered a prototype weapon that outperformed all the others. On September 30, 1941, the Ordnance Department recommended standardization of the Winchester model. The recommendation was approved, and the new weapon was given the designation Carbine, Caliber .30, M1. Ammunition was fed to the gun via a detachable 15-round box magazine.

Winchester was already busy with a number of other important projects when it won the design competition for the new carbine. Knowing that Winchester could never build enough M1 carbines to fill the army's requirements, the Ordnance Department bought the manufacturing rights from the company and gave production contracts for the weapon to the General Motor's Inland Manufacturing Division on November 24, 1941, and many others. As the army dramatically increased in size after the Japanese attack on Pearl Harbor, the Ordnance Department brought additional companies into the program. By war's end, over 10 companies were involved in building over six million M1 carbines and their variations.

In combat use, the M1 carbine received mixed reactions. Soldiers appreciated its light weight and compact shape but decried its lack of stopping power. In a wartime report, an American soldier commented: "The carbine is

Pictured in the hands of a U.S. Army soldier in World War II is a Submachine Gun, Caliber .45, Thompson, M1A1. Notice the cocking handle (actuator) slot is now on the right side of the weapon's receiver. Other changes included replacing the finely finished barrel cooling fins found on the M1928A1 model with a plain steel barrel and discarding the compensator at the muzzle. *National Archives*

Infantry Weapons 23

Posing for the photographer in this World War II picture is an American tanker holding a Submachine Gun, Caliber .45, M3. Most American soldiers knew the weapon by its popular nickname the "grease gun." Clearly visible is the weapon's cocking handle on the right side of the receiver housing assembly. In the improved M3A1 version of the grease gun the bolt was pulled to the rear with a finger to cock the gun. *National Archives*

Submachine Guns

One of the best-known infantry weapons to come out of World War II was the Thompson submachine gun. The history of this famous weapon dates back to 1917, when a U.S. Army Ordnance officer named John Taliaferro Thompson first conceived of a compact full-automatic weapon firing the short-range .45-caliber pistol cartridge. Up until that point in time the army had shown little or no interest in such a weapon.

Thompson, who coined the term "submachine gun," envisioned his weapon as being suitable for use by infantrymen in close-combat and by law enforcement personnel. Fellow Ordnance Department officers as well as a number of navy officers expressed interest in Thompson's concept, leading him to believe that he had a viable invention.

Despite Thompson's early efforts to interest the American military in the subject of submachine guns, it was the Italian and German armies that introduced the first submachine guns into combat in 1918. The Italian weapon was built by Beretta and called the Villar Perosa. The German weapon was built by the Bergmann and designated the MP 18. (In German military terminology the letters "MP" stood for machine pistol).

To market his proposed submachine gun after World War I Thompson (by then retired) went to the Auto-Ordnance Corporation. In 1920 the company submitted to the Ordnance Department and the Marine Corps a prototype weapon based on Thompson's design for testing. The tests went so well that Auto-Ordnance optimistically decided to contract in 1921 with a number of firms (including Colt) to supply components for at least 15,000 weapons that it would then assemble. The production weapon was designated the Thompson Submachine Gun, Model of 1921. It fired from either a detachable 20-round box magazine or a detachable 50-round drum magazine.

The early production models of the M1921 impressed both the Ordnance Department and the Marine Corps during firing trials. Despite its excellent showing however, neither armed service placed orders for the weapon. Sadly for Thompson and his company, he could have not picked a worse time to market a new infantry weapon. With the end of World War I the U.S. Army and most of the other armies of the world, reverted back to much smaller peacetime levels, leaving storage warehouses packed full of perfectly useful infantry weapons.

The war-weary American public and its political leaders had dubbed World War I "the war to

definitely not liked because of its numerous stoppages. Also the slug has very little impact and killing ability, or power."

Two modified versions of the M1 carbine were introduced into service by the Ordnance Department during World War II, the M1A1 and the M2. The M1A1 carbine, adopted into service in May 1942, was identical to the M1 version except for a folding stock. It was intended for use by the army's airborne forces where compactness was of key importance. The M2 version of the M1 carbine was capable of both full automatic and semiautomatic fire but was not introduced into service until after the war in Europe ended. The key visual clue that identifies the M2 carbine was the selector switch on the left side of the receiver.

A pint-sized American soldier armed with an M3 grease gun poses for a photographer in this World War II picture. After a small arms weapon is cocked, firing is initiated by squeezing a trigger. This movement trips the sear, releasing the firing mechanism (firing pin, hammer or, in automatic weapons, such parts as the bolt group or slide), causing it to move forward with enough force to discharge the round. *National Archives*

Chapter One   25

end all wars." Buying a new infantry weapon, no matter how promising, was out of the question in the early 1920s. Efforts by Auto-Ordnance to interest foreign armies in acquiring the weapon also failed to generate any sales.

As the Auto-Ordnance Corporation struggled to stay solvent in its early years, its product soon acquired a notoriety that persists until this day. This notoriety was acquired in the 1920s when a handful of American criminals began using the M1921 in their illegal activities. This fact caught the attention of the press of the day, which nicknamed the weapon the "tommy gun," and printed sensational stories about it use. (The Auto-Ordnance Corporation eventually patented the term "Tommy Gun.") The American motion picture industry added to the mystique of the weapon by producing movies that incorrectly portrayed every criminal in America being armed with an M1921

The American soldier pictured has taped three of the grease gun's 30-round detachable box magazines together for easier reloading. The grease gun, like the various versions of the Thompson, was a blowback-operated weapon. With such mechanisms the initial blow of the exploding cartridge started the bolt moving rearward, but the weight of the bolt is such that it did not allow the chamber to be entirely opened until the round has left the bore. Action by a recoil spring returned the bolt to the closed position, chambering a new round.
National Archives

equipped with a 50- or 100-round detachable drum magazine. In response, American law enforcement agencies began adding the M1921 to their inventory of small arms.

It was not until 1928 that the Auto-Ordnance Corporation received it first official military order for the M1921. The small order for 500 weapons came not from the U.S. Army but from the U.S. Navy, ordering on behalf of the Marine Corps. The navy insisted on some minor modifications to the weapon before taking it into service, resulting in the new designation U.S. Navy, Model of 1928.

The army did not express any official interest in the M1921 until the early 1930s. It was at this time that the army acquired a small number. The need arose when the cavalry branch began trading in its horses for wheeled and tracked armored vehicles. Some within the cavalry branch believed that the compact M1921 (32 inches long) would be the perfect choice as a self-defense weapon for the crews of armored vehicles, if they forced to leave their vehicles in combat. Others within the cavalry branch preferred waiting until the M1 semiautomatic rifle entered service. The infantry branch continued to see no need for the weapon.

The cavalry branch concluded in 1937 that the M1 semiautomatic rifle was too long (43.6 inches) to be stored within the confined spaces of armored vehicles. The M1921 was now seen as the more logical choice. However, it took the German invasion of Poland on September 10, 1939, before the Ordnance Department got around to ordering 950 additional examples of the M1921 (newly designated as the Submachine Gun, Caliber .45, Model of 1928A1). Like the earlier M1921 and M1928 Navy model, the M1928A1 could be fired from either a detachable 20-round box magazine or a 50-round detachable drum magazine.

The French government, also worried about the threat posed by German aggression in Europe, ordered almost 4,000 Model 1921 guns from Auto-Ordnance in 1939. These orders, and the anticipation of more to come, led Auto-Ordnance to arrange with the Savage Arms Company to build its product under license.

The successful German invasion of both the Low Countries and France motivated the Ordnance Department in late 1940 to place an order for 20,000 more of the M1928A1. By 1941, weapons ordered jumped to over 300,000, with the great majority being sent via Lend-Lease to Great Britain. Due to the German submarine campaign, over half of the guns shipped to England ended up, unused, at the bottom of the Atlantic Ocean. The U.S. Army remained cool to deploying large numbers of the M1928A1, preferring to await the arrival of the newly developed M1 Carbine. After the Japanese sneak attack on Pearl Harbor, the army decided it would need both weapons in large numbers as quickly as possible.

In response to the large increase in orders for the M1928A1 from the army the Auto-Ordnance Corporation progressively introduced into the weapon's assembly line a series of features aimed at simplifying its design to speed up its production and save on raw materials. The M1928A1 would be produced until early 1943, with over 550,000 manufactured. It was then gradually replaced in production by a simpler version of the weapon redesigned by a Savage engineering team. This redesigned weapon was designated the Submachine Gun, Caliber .45, M1. Roughly 290,000 such guns were made between early 1942 and early 1943.

Unlike the earlier version of the Thompson, the M1 could not accept the original detachable drum magazines. To make up for this loss of capacity, a new 30-round detachable box magazine was developed. While the earlier versions of the Thompson employed a delayed blowback operating system, the M1 and its successor used a straight blowback operating system.

After the M1 entered production, the engineering team at Savage did itself one better and managed to incorporate into the weapon's design even further simplifications in its construction. This version of the weapon was designated the Submachine Gun, Caliber .45, M1A1, which began full-scale production in early 1943. When production of the M1A1 ended in late 1944, over 500,000 examples had been built. In addition, many original M1 versions were converted into the M1A1 configuration.

Despite the army's desire to see the various versions of the Thompson submachine gun restricted to use by specialized troops, such as

Two American soldiers are pictured ready to fire their M1917A1 .30-caliber machine gun. The official designation was Gun, Machine, Caliber .30, Browning, M1917A1. Like so many other machine guns put into service before and during World War I, the American weapon was water-cooled, as evident by the circular metal water jacket around the barrel of the weapon. The M1917A1 fired ball and armor-piercing (AP) ammunition at a muzzle velocity of 2,800 feet per second. The weapon's maximum range was 3,500 yards. *National Archives*

Chapter One   27

paratroopers, armored infantrymen, or army rangers. The weapon was extremely popular with the average infantryman, who saw its possession as a status symbol and acquired one by whatever means possible.

American troops equipped with the Thompson often complained about its weight—10.45 pounds. An ammunition pouch with eight loaded 20-round magazines weighed an additional 10 pounds. On the other hand, they tended to be very pleased with its use in combat. A U.S. Army officer commented in a report: "The TSMG [Thompson submachine gun] is a favorite weapon for close-in fighting. It has a good rate of fire and excellent stopping power against attacking dismounted troops."

The Ordnance Department was never happy with the Thompson. It appeared in widespread army service only because it was the sole American-made submachine in mass production at the beginning of World War II. Despite the various design efforts aimed at simplifying the Thompson, the Ordnance Department believed the weapon took too long to build and was too costly. Due to the era in which the Thompson was designed, little thought had been given to ease of assembly or other cost-cutting measures in its construction. Building the Thompson required specialized machine tools and highly trained machinists.

In early 1941 the Ordnance Department began to look for a more suitable submachine gun that would be simpler and less costly to build than the various versions of the Thompson. The weapon eventually selected for production in June 1942 by the Marlin Firearms Company was designated the U.S. Submachine Gun, Caliber .45, M2. George J. Hyde designed it. A host of startup problems with the M2 forced the Ordnance Department to cancel its contract for the weapon.

During World War II, the M1917A1 .30-caliber machine gun was found at the battalion level of infantry units in the heavy-weapons company. The word "heavy" was a relative term only. In fact, the M1917A1 could be hand-carried, as can be seen in this picture, for considerable distances at a reasonable walking speed. It was considered heavy only because it was less mobile when compared to the weapons use in a U.S. Army rifle company. *National Archives*

The Ordnance Department again took up the search for a suitable submachine gun. George Hyde took this opportunity to submit a totally new weapon that was designed for cheap mass production with unskilled labor. The Ordnance Department liked what they saw and authorized its production by General Motor's Guide Lamp Division in December 1942. The blowback-operated weapon was designated the Submachine Gun, Caliber .45, M3. The weapon was soon nicknamed the "grease gun," due to its resemblance to the tool used for lubricating automobiles of the era.

The M3 fired from a 30-round detachable box magazine. As designed, it could only be fired in full automatic mode; however, some American soldiers, taking advantage of the weapon's slow rate of fire, could actually fire single rounds when need be.

The initial reaction of American soldiers who first saw the all-metal M3 in late 1943 was less than enthusiastic. It did not have the conventional wooden stock and handgrip found on the various models of the Thompson. Instead, it had only a retractable skeleton wire stock. In addition to its unconventional appearance that put off so many soldiers, there were also a number of minor design problems with the early production M3s. Once these problems were corrected, the M3 was gradually accepted by American soldiers as equal to or better than the Thompson in some regards, such as weight and accuracy. By war's end over 600,000 M3s came off American production lines.

In April 1944 the Ordnance Department decided to incorporate some additional design changes into the M3 to increase its combat effectiveness as well as speeding up its production. The improved version of the M3 was designated in December 1944 as the Submachine Gun, Caliber .45, M3A1. Roughly 15,000 examples of the M3A1 were built before the war ended. Few saw combat use in World War II.

Machine Guns

During World War II the U.S. Army employed two basic types of machine guns, the smaller one being .30 caliber and the larger one .50 caliber. Both machine guns came from the fertile genius of America's best-known arms designer, John M. Browning.

Browning had decided at the beginning of the twentieth century that what the U.S. Army would need for the future was a recoil-operated, water-cooled machine gun. His first step was the invention of a successful recoil operating mechanism that he patented in 1901. Since the army had not yet identified the need for a new recoil-operated machine gun, Browning discontinued work on the project until he knew it would be needed.

By 1916 many Americans, including Browning, believed it was only a matter of time until the country was drawn into World War I. He therefore finished work on his prototype recoil-operated, water-cooled machine gun, chambered to fire the army's standard .30-06-caliber service round. He then arranged for a series of firing demonstrations for interested parties in early 1917. The Ordnance Department soon arranged for its own test of the weapon at the Springfield Armory. The performance of Browning's .30-caliber machine gun was so impressive that the army decided to adopt the weapon on the spot. It was assigned the designation Caliber .30 Browning Machine Gun Model 1917.

The M1917A1 .30-caliber machine gun, pictured at maximum firing elevation, was fired from the M1917A1 lightweight (53.4-pounds) portable folding mount. The mount had as a central member a socket with three projecting lugs. Attached to these lugs were three legs, which could be clamped independently in various positions. The cradle assembly sat in the socket and housed the elevating and traversing mechanism. *National Archives*

Remington, Colt, and the New England Westinghouse Corporation undertook production of the M1917 to fill the army's needs. The three companies managed to complete almost 70,000 guns before the war ended.

As the army started to rebuild in the late 1930s, the Ordnance Department decided to make some minor improvements to the World War I-era M1917s still in the inventory. Reflecting these changes to the basic design, the army redesignated the weapon as the M1917A1. To keep up with demand, the Ordnance Department contracted with a number of civilian firms to build over 50,000 new examples of the M1917A1 during World War II.

The biggest drawback with the M1917A1 was its overall weight. The gun (with water added) weighed in at 41 pounds. The tripod added another 53.4 pounds. In addition, the three-man crew had to carry the weapon's water and ammunition cans, plus a number of minor accessories. To address this problem the Ordnance Department began looking into a much lighter air-cooled version of the weapon as early as the 1920s.

It took until the mid-1930s before the Ordnance Department came up with a satisfactory air-cooled version of Browning's .30-caliber machine gun. The new air-cooled version was designated the M1919A4. It featured a perforated barrel-cooling jacket that brought the gun's weight down to 31 pounds. The gun was mounted on the newly designed M2 tripod that weighed only 14 pounds. Almost 400,000 examples of the M1919A4 were manufactured by a variety of civilian firms during World War II.

Despite the age of the Browning's basic design, it performed well in combat. An army officer commented in a World War II report about his opinion of the weapon's effectiveness:

"The American .30 Cal. M.G. [machine gun] is considered one of the best weapons we have. Its rate of fire is sufficient. It is a well-built weapon and very dependable under the toughest conditions."

Combat experience soon convinced American front-line combat troops that they needed a new light machine gun that would fall somewhere between the 20-pound BAR and the 45-pound

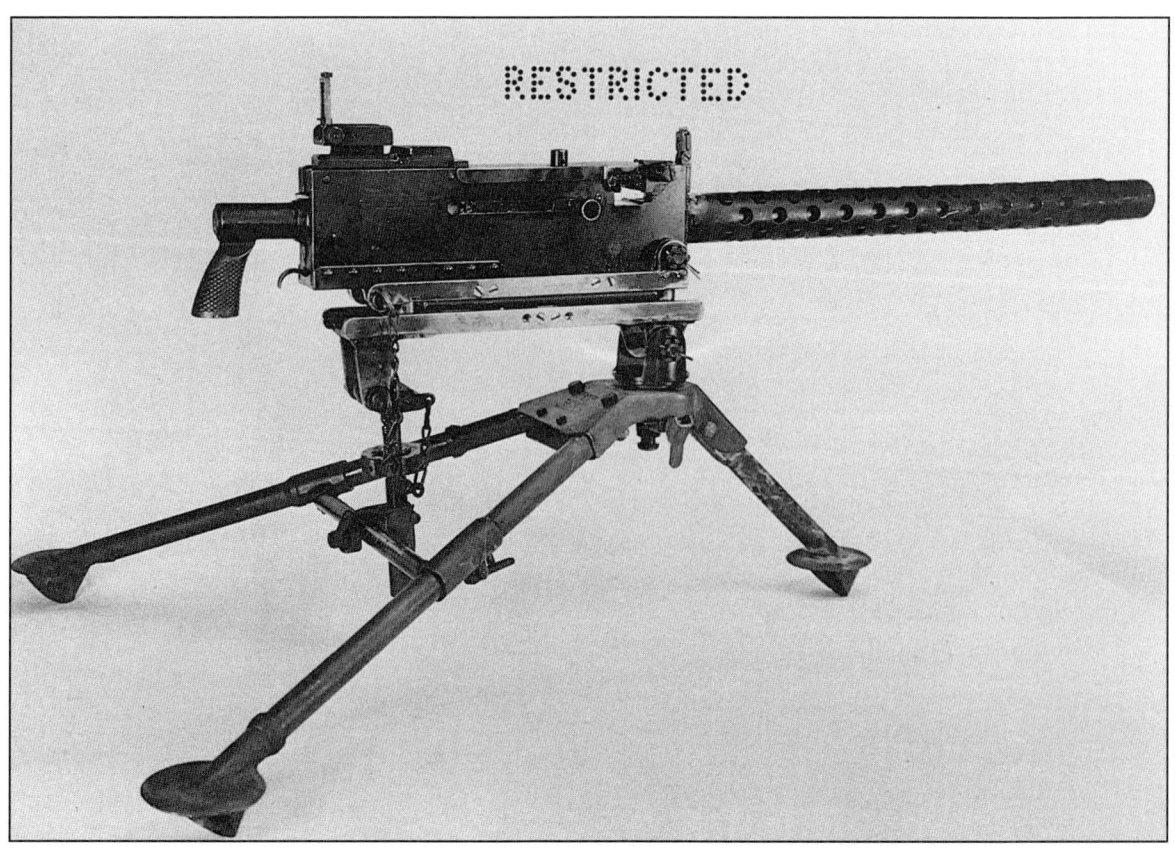

The M1919A4 .30-caliber machine gun was normally fired from the lightweight folding tripod M2. It consisted of three tubular steel legs articulating in a tripod head, the two rear legs being joined and additionally supported by a traversing bar forming a simple A-truss, which served as a rear support for the elevating mechanism, which in turn supported the mounted gun. *National Archives*

An American soldier armed with an air-cooled M1919A4 .30-caliber machine gun gives the photographer a big smile. During World War II, each U.S. Army rifle company had a weapons platoon which contained the unit's crew-served weapons. The weapons platoon had two sections, one of which was armed with two M1919A4 machine guns. The other section had three 60-mm mortars. This made up the organic fire support of the infantry company, giving a company commander the means to closely support his three rifle platoons. *National Archives*

(with tripod) M1919A4. The Ordnance Department knew that there was no time to develop a new light machine gun from the ground up. So a decision was made to modify the existing M1919A4 design to serve that role.

The new version of the Browning .30-caliber machine gun was designated the M1919A6. It featured a lighter barrel, as well as a pistol grip and carrying handle. In place of the M2 tripod the M1919A6 had a detachable shoulder stock and a front-mounted bipod. With all the above weight-saving efforts, the Ordnance Department managed to push the weight of the 1919A6 down to a more manageable 32.5 pounds, making it 12.5 pounds lighter than the M1919A4 mounted on its tripod. American industry would produce a little over 40,000 of the M1919A6s during World War II.

The largest machine gun in U.S. Army service during World War II was a very powerful and hard-hitting .50-caliber weapon. Browning initially developed it during World War I in response to an Ordnance Department request for a machine gun able to fire a newly developed .50-caliber cartridge. It was envisioned that the new machine gun would be used as an antitank weapon. Browning had a prototype ready for testing in late 1918, but the war ended before it could be placed into production. Browning's design for his new .50-caliber machine gun was a scaled-up version of his .30-caliber M1917 machine gun including a water-cooled barrel.

After World War I, work continued on improving the .50-caliber cartridge as well as the machine gun designed to fire it. Tests conducted by the Ordnance Department beginning in 1919 confirmed that both the ammunition and gun met all the needed requirements for toughness and reliability. Both the U.S. Army and Navy soon adopted it as the .50-caliber Model 1921.

Due to a lack of money, neither service could afford to buy many of the M1921 guns until 1929. A slightly improved version of the weapon, designated the M1921A1, was adopted

The crew of an early model .50-caliber M2 Heavy Barrel (HB) Machine Gun is using a small telescope sight for aiming the weapon. By repositioning some of the component parts, the gun was capable of alternate feed (ammunition could be fed from either the right or left side of the receiver). However, under most circumstances, the gun was fed from the left side. A disintegrating metallic link belt was used in feeding. In preparation for firing, the first round required manual operation. *National Archives*

A young American army officer is pictured firing a M1919A6 .30-caliber machine gun from the prone position. Clearly visible is the folding bipod at the front end of the barrel jacket as well as the detachable shoulder stock at the rear of the receiver. Near the rear of the barrel jacket is a carrying handle. If required, the M1919A6 could be fired from the M1917A1 tripod mount as well as the M2 tripod mount. *National Archives*

in 1930. While the M1921 and the M1921A1 could be mounted on a tripod for infantry use, the weight of gun with water (121 pounds) generally confined it to static role as a rear area antiaircraft weapon. Both versions of the M1921 were declared obsolete during World War II and pulled from service.

While the coast artillery branch of the U.S. Army was somewhat pleased with the water-cooled versions of Browning's .50 caliber machine guns, the Army Air Corps, as well as the cavalry and infantry branches still lacked what the Chief of Ordnance described as "suitably specialized Brownings."

The Air Corps needed a lightweight air-cooled .50-caliber machine gun that could be fed from either side of the receiver. The cavalry wanted an air-cooled .50-caliber machine gun that could be mounted on tanks and other armored fighting vehicles. The infantry wanted an air-cooled .50-caliber machine gun that could be fired from a tripod and still light enough to be carried into combat by ground troops if the need arose.

None of the various services nor the Ordnance Department believed that it would be possible to have a single air-cooled .50-caliber machine gun that could serve such diverse purposes. But, in a span of only two years

An American soldier is aiming a .50-caliber M2 Heavy Barrel (HB) Machine Gun, mounted on the rear of a jeep, at an imaginary aerial target. Air-cooling of the weapon's barrel was permitted through maximum exposure to the air of the barrel and receiver. Perforations in the barrel support allowed air to circulate around the breech end of the barrel and help to cool the parts. The heavy barrel was used to retard early overheating. *National Archives*

Pictured is a tank-mounted .50-caliber M2 Heavy Barrel (HB) Machine Gun. It could be fired by the vehicle commander in an antiaircraft role from the safety of the tank's turret. For use against ground targets the vehicle commander had to stand outside the vehicle's turret to make effective use of the weapon, leaving him highly exposed to return fire. *National Archives*

(1931–1933) Dr. Samuel G. Green of the Ordnance Department succeeded in modifying the design of Browning's weapon to make a single weapon which met the requirements for all the using services. This new model of Browning's original design was put into service in 1933 and designated the Caliber .50 Browning Machine Gun, Heavy Barrel (HB), M2. It was easily recognizable because it had no perforated, full-length metal tube enclosing the barrel as did the air-cooled barrel on the .30 caliber Browning machine guns.

The M2 HB was designed so that the operating mechanism was the same for each type of gun. The heavy barrel of the tank-mounted gun, the water-filled barrel of the antiaircraft gun, and the lighter parts of the aircraft gun could each be attached without modification of the weapon's receiver. This design feature pioneered by Dr. Green allowed the simplification of the manufacturing process, maintenance, and troop training.

By the end of World War II, various civilian manufacturers under contract to the Ordnance Department managed to build over two million guns of the M2 HB design. The great majority of these were allocated for use on aircraft. The remaining weapons were divided between an infantry air-cooled version designated the .50 HB Flex (Heavy Barrel, Flexible) of which roughly 350,000 were built, and a water-cooled antiaircraft version, of which a little more than 80,000 were built. The water-cooled version of the M2 was declared obsolete near the end of World War II, with all the remaining examples being converted into the M2 HB version.

Mounted on a variety of military vehicles or used on a tripod, the M2 HB was extremely effective against exposed infantry or lightly armored or nonarmored wheeled and tracked vehicles. A tank crew who commented in a wartime report summed up the general opinion of most American soldiers who use the M2 HB in combat by stating: "Our .50-cal. machine gun is tops."

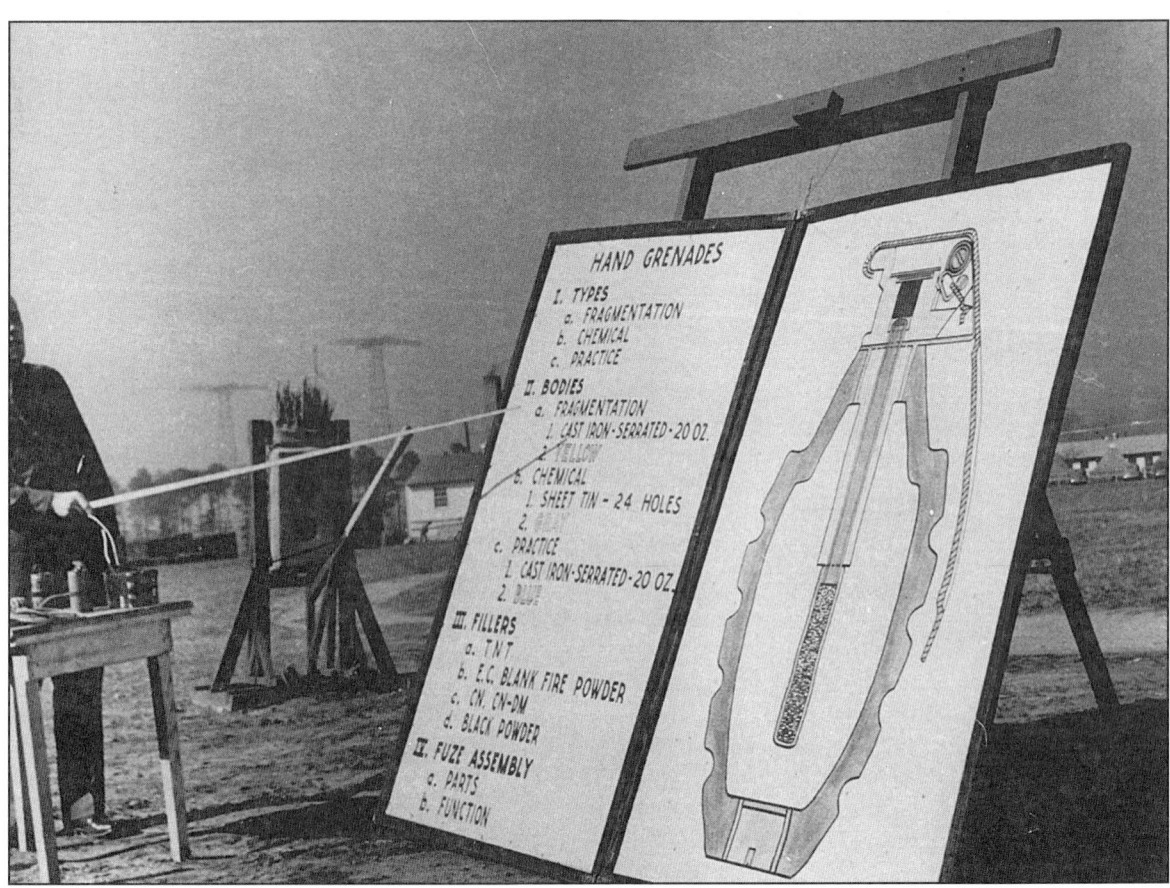

A U.S. Army instructor points to a large cut-away diagram of a hand grenade during a training class. The effective casualty radius of a hand grenade is relatively small when compared to other weapons. Effective casualty radius is defined by the military as the radius of a circular area around the point of detonation within which at least 50 percent of the exposed personnel will become casualties. The effective casualty radius varies with the type of grenade used. *National Archives*

Grenades and Grenade Launchers

Another infantry weapon that saw a great deal of use with the U.S. Army in both Worlds War I and II was the hand grenade. A hand grenade is nothing more than a small hand-thrown bomb. It comes in many different sizes, shapes, and types that are designed to fulfill a wide variety of purposes. They can be used for inflicting material and personnel casualties; for screening, signaling, and illuminating; for demolition and harassing, and for incendiary affect.

The range of a hand grenade has always been relatively short; depended on the ability of the individual thrower and the shape of the grenade. A well-trained soldier could throw the army's standard World War II fragmentation hand grenade, the Mark II, (which weighted about 21 ounces) an average of 44 yards. With the larger M15 white phosphorus grenade (which weighted 31 ounces) the average soldier would be lucky to reach a distance of 27 yards.

To extend the range of its grenades in World War I, the Ordnance Department copied a French army grenade launcher known as the Vivien Bessier. It would remain in service with the U.S. Army until the 1920s, when the M1 and M2 grenade launchers replaced it in service. Both grenade launchers, as with the original French model, clamped on the end of a rifle's barrel, and increased the range of the grenade to approximately 165 yards.

The M1 grenade launcher was designed for use with the Springfield rifle and the M2 with the Enfield. Very few M2 grenade launchers saw use with American soldiers during World War II because the Enfield was employed mainly as a training weapon. The M1 grenade launcher, in contrast, saw heavy use until the end of the war.

As the M1 rifle and the M1 carbine replaced the Springfield rifle in service, the Ordnance Department had to design grenade launchers

American soldiers were taught that for the greatest degree of accuracy and range, a grenade should be thrown like a baseball, using the throwing motion most natural to the individual. The picture shows a soldier who has already pulled the safety pin of his grenade and has cocked his throwing arm to the rear. After a grenade was thrown, soldiers were instructed to observe the target point to confirm its impact, then duck their heads to avoid fragments or other effects. *National Archives*

for the new weapons. The M1 rifle received the M7 G grenade launcher and the M1 Carbine the M8 grenade launcher.

The M7 Grenade Launcher was not a complete success in combat, due to fact that once it was fitted to the M1 rifle, the weapon could no longer function in its semiautomatic mode. This design fault was the reason that many Springfield rifles fitted with the M1 grenade launchers survived in service for so long.

The various types of grenade launchers employed by the U.S. Army during World War II were used to fire a variety of rounds. The most important was the M9A1 antitank rifle grenade. An earlier version designated the M9 was only in brief service at the beginning of the war until replaced by the M9A1. Another round was designated the M17 impact fragmentation grenade; it was a standard Mark II fragmentation grenade attached to an adapter, which held it in place when fitted to the grenade launcher. In addition, there was white phosphorus (WP) as well as a number of colored smoke rifle grenades.

Bazooka

A novel type of weapon that appeared in the U.S. Army inventory during World War II was an antitank rocket launcher, better known to most soldiers by its popular nickname the "bazooka." The term "bazooka" came from the resemblance it had to a strange-looking musical instrument invented by Bob Burns, a well-known radio comedian of the day.

In its original form, the bazooka was one of the simplest weapons ever produced by the Ordnance Department. It weighed about 18 pounds and consisted of nothing more than a 54-inch steel tube of 2.36-inch inside diameter, open at both ends. Along the bottom of the tube were two handgrips, the rear grip containing the trigger and electrical contact switches. A wooden shoulder stock located behind the rear grip contained two dry-cell flashlight-type batteries. One of the batteries provided the electrical current necessary to set off a 3.4-pound, fin-stabilized rocket inserted into the rear end of the weapon. The other battery was a spare. A front sight was

An American soldier preparing to launch an M9A1 rifle grenade from an M7 grenade launcher mounted on the end of his M1 Garand semiautomatic rifle. The grenade launcher was composed of a sleeve (tube), having a series of annular rings around its periphery attached to a bracket. With the grenade in place on the launcher the rings were used in conjunction with the angle of elevation to determine range. *National Archives*

at the muzzle end of the weapon. The rear sight was nothing more than a simple metal leaf.

Leslie A. Skinner of the Ordnance Department came up with the prototype design for the bazooka in early 1942. After finding a suitable warhead for his rocket, Skinner and his assistant demonstrated their new invention to some high-ranking army officers. One of the officers present at the demonstration was the head of the Ordnance Department's Research and Development (R&D) program. He was so impressed with what he saw that he ordered Skinner's device into full-scale production directly. The strange new weapon was officially standardized in June 1942 as the Launcher, Rocket AT (Antitank) M1. The rocket fired from the M1 bazooka was designated the M6.

General Electric was given 30 days by the Ordnance Department to build over 5,000 bazookas. Of those 30 days GE had to spend nearly half in making working models for testing purposes. It took until the 14th model of the bazooka before GE won approval for series

The 2.36-inch rocket launcher M1 was a smoothbore, breech-loading shoulder weapon of the open tube type. It could be fired from the standing, kneeling, sitting, or prone position. When fired there was little recoil, since the propulsion of the rocket was accomplished by the jet action of the propellant power in the stabilizer tube of the rocket and did not depend upon gas pressure built up inside the launcher tube. *National Archives*

An American soldier sliding a 2.36-inch rocket into the rear of an M1 rocket-launcher. The M1 rocket launcher was better known to all by its nickname the "bazooka." Because of the considerable back blast from such weapons when fired, it was stressed in training that no personnel or inflammable material be directly behind the launcher within a distance of 25 yards to prevent being burned by the rocket propellant. *National Archives*

Chapter One   37

production from the Ordnance Department. GE met the deadline imposed by the Ordnance Department with only 89 minutes to spare. While GE was building the first production bazookas, the E. G. Company was making 25,000 M6 rockets.

Anticipating the need for even more bazookas, the Ordnance Department asked GE to build another 60,000 examples in 1942. In 1943, bazookas requested went up to 100,000, and in 1944 that number grew to 200,000. By the end of World War II, GE had managed to build almost 450,000 bazookas of various types. The Cheney Bigelow Wire Works Company contributed another 40,000 bazookas late in the war.

An American soldier poses with a 2.36-inch M1 rocket launcher and a captured example of its much larger and more powerful German cousin, the 8.8-centimeter (3.46-inch) Raketenpanzerbueches. The German rocket launcher was based on examples of the American weapon captured in North Africa in early 1943. Since the rocket motor on the German weapon was still burning when it left the launcher tube, a small shield (as seen in this picture) was fitted to the front of the weapon to protect the soldier pulling the trigger. *National Archives*

The army's early combat experience with the bazooka was not particularly impressive. A number of early production models were hastily supplied to the troops taking part in the American invasion of French North Africa (November 1942). With no time to become familiar with the new weapon the troops had little confidence in it. On the evening before the troops boarded the ships that were to take them to North Africa, General Dwight Eisenhower, commander of the invasion forces, was shocked when one of his troop commanders told him that he was completely at a loss "as to how to teach his men the use of this vitally needed weapon." He said, "I don't know anything about it myself except from hearsay."

A number of design problems cropped up with the bazookas in the field due to the haste in which they were produced. Most of the problems were related to the batteries and the unreliable M6 rocket. Consequently, it did not play an important part in the fighting in North Africa. There were so many reports of malfunctions that the War Department suspended further issue of the weapon in May 1943. A high-ranking army general visiting the North African theater of operation at the end of the fighting could not find anyone who could say definitely that a tank had been stopped by bazooka fire.

During the American invasion of Sicily in July 1943, the early-model M1 bazooka launcher with the M6 rocket was given another chance at proving itself in combat. The Ordnance Department had hoped to deploy a new improved model (the M1A1 launcher and M6A1 rocket) for the invasion, but it did not reach the area in time. Instead, the new version of the bazooka would be saved for the invasion of Europe planned for mid-1944.

Due to its poor showing during the fighting in North Africa, the early-model bazooka's performance was watched very closely. One Ordnance Department observer in Sicily claimed that bazookas accounted for at least four German medium tanks, and at least one German heavy Tiger tank, though admittedly the tank was knocked out by a lucky hit through the driver's vision slot. Despite the bazooka's limited success against a small number of German tanks in Sicily, most American soldiers preferred the M9A1 rifle grenade as a close-range antitank weapon. The main redeeming feature of the bazooka that won over the American soldiers fighting in Sicily

38   *Infantry Weapons*

was its deadly effectiveness against enemy defensive emplacements. The bazooka was now thought of more than just an antitank weapon and was soon in high demand.

Patton expressed his thoughts regarding the bazooka in a letter of instruction to his senior commanders on May 20, 1944:

"The purpose of the bazooka is not to hunt tanks offensively, but to be used as the last resort in keeping tanks from overrunning infantry. Since the bazooka is unarmored, and always discloses its position when fired, it must get a hit on the first shot. To insure this, the range should be held to around 30 yards. When thus used, the bazooka will hit and penetrate any tank that I have yet seen and will probably stop it. If used at longer ranges, it will probably miss and its operators will then become targets for the tank's machine guns."

In late 1943 the Ordnance Department, at the request of the Airborne Command, developed a new version of the bazooka designated the M9A1. Unlike the long and cumbersome launcher tubes of the earlier model bazookas, the launcher tube on the M9A1 could be broken down into two separate parts for ease of transport. The Ordnance Department also improved upon the design of the M6A1 rocket and came up with a more powerful version designated the M6A3 rocket.

Despite various improvements to the bazooka design and the rockets it fired, it would prove unequal to the demands placed upon it during the fighting in Western Europe in 1944 and 1945. An example of the disappointment felt by American soldiers regarding the performance of the bazooka can be found in a late war report, which contained the comments of Corporal Donald E. Lewis:

"The German bazooka is by far superior to the American bazooka. In a test between the two, the German bazooka penetrated two bogie wheels and also the side of a Mark V [Panther] tank. It is also left dents on the other side of the tank. Much hot steel was spattered around inside. It also penetrated the front slope plate leaving about a half or quarter inch hole. The American bazooka was fired at the same range. It hit the top of one bogie wheel and failed to penetrate the sides of the tank. The second shot hit the broad side of the tank just above the bogie wheel and left a hole that would barely let light through. It entirely failed to penetrate the front slope plate. The concussion effect of the German bazooka is at the least double that of ours. I was so favorably impressed that I was ready to take after the Krauts [Germans] with their own weapon. I will guarantee that I was not alone in my feelings."

To overcome the 2.36-inch bazooka's lack of tank-killing ability, the Ordnance Department began to work on a 3.5-inch bazooka firing a much larger and more powerful rocket in October 1944. Unfortunately the fruits of this labor did not appear until after World War II.

A proud American soldier armed with an M9A1 rocket launcher poses in front of the German medium tank he destroyed with his bazooka. It took a brave man to stalk and destroy a tank. German tanks normally operated in conjunction with other armored vehicles and supporting infantry. The rocket fired from the bazooka weighed 3.4-pounds and was supposed to penetrate almost 5 inches of steel armor under the right conditions. *National Archives*

Chapter One 39

Chapter Two

ARTILLERY WEAPONS

After his success in leading the charge across Western Europe in 1944-45 with the armored divisions of his beloved Third Army, Patton was the first to admit: "I don't have to tell you who won the war, you know our artillery did." Patton knew full well that many major successes of the Third Army were owed to the artillery branch's support of the tank and infantry branches.

Indeed, the Germans feared the artillery branch the most and credited it for their eventual defeat. General Dwight D. Eisenhower stated after the war: "The speed, accuracy and devastating power of

A heavy artillery piece used by the U.S. Army during World War I was the Vickers Mark VI 8-inch howitzer, seen here in use with the British army in December 1916. The various versions of the British howitzer could fire a 200-pound high-explosive shell to a maximum range of 12,300 yards. Rushed into production by the British army in the early stages of World War I, it would soldier on into World War II. *National Archives*

American artillery won confidence and admiration from the troops it supported and inspired fear and respect in their enemy." Napoleon neatly summed up the beliefs of artillerymen throughout history by stating, "God fights on the side with the best artillery."

The victories enjoyed by the artillery branch of the U.S. Army had not come easily, and there were many missteps along the way. When the American government decided in April 1917 to join England and France against the Germans during World War I, the U.S. Army's inventory of artillery was found wanting. This was primarily due to the army's prewar neglect of its field artillery. (Field artillery is the mobile element that accompanies the infantry into battle). When it arrived in France in 1917, the U.S. Army was forced to go into battle with foreign field artillery guns, howitzers, and mortars.

The American army took a number of heavy British towed artillery pieces into service during World War I. Among the various British-made

Another foreign artillery piece that saw widespread service with the U.S. Army in World War I was the famous French-designed 75-mm Mle 1897 gun. Pictured is an American-built copy of the French gun on outside display at the U.S. Army Ordnance Museum at Aberdeen Proving Ground, Maryland. In American service it was nicknamed the "French 75." It fired a 12-pound high-explosive shell to a maximum range of 7,500 yards. *National Archives*

To fill the gap between the British heavy 8-inch howitzer and the light "French 75," the U.S. Army adopted the French-designed 155-mm Mle 1917 into service during World War I. In American service the 155-mm howitzer was designated the M1917. It fired a 95-pound high-explosive shell to a maximum range of 12,400 yards. *National Archives*

Chapter Two   41

Artillery Definitions

The term "gun" encompasses all classes of firearms. In its military definition, gun applies to a cannon (a general term encompassing all artillery pieces) with a relatively long barrel fired from a carriage or fixed mount. Guns have long barrels, high muzzle velocities and flat trajectories below 45 degrees. Artillery pieces classified as guns are generally used for long-range, indirect fire.

A howitzer is a comparatively short cannon with a medium muzzle velocity. Howitzers are usually fired at relatively steep elevations so the rounds can reach targets hidden from flat-trajectory guns. Variations in the propelling charge change a round's trajectory and range. The howitzer's range lies between the gun and the mortar.

Sometimes the distinction between an artillery gun and a howitzer becomes blurred due to the development of gun-howitzers that can perform both roles. The best-known Allied gun-howitzer used during World War II was the British 25-Pounder Gun, which had a caliber of 87-mm.

Mortars are cannons with short, usually smoothbore, barrels and with very low muzzle velocities. They are almost always fired at very steep elevations. Like howitzers, graded charges can vary the trajectory of a round. Mortars are used at short range to reach nearby targets that are protected or concealed by intervening hills or other barriers.

Because mortars have short barrels, they tend to be light in weight. In smaller calibers, they are man-portable and are supplied to infantry units in all armies. Moreover, unlike larger and heavier artillery guns and howitzers, man-portable mortars do not require trained specialists to be effective.

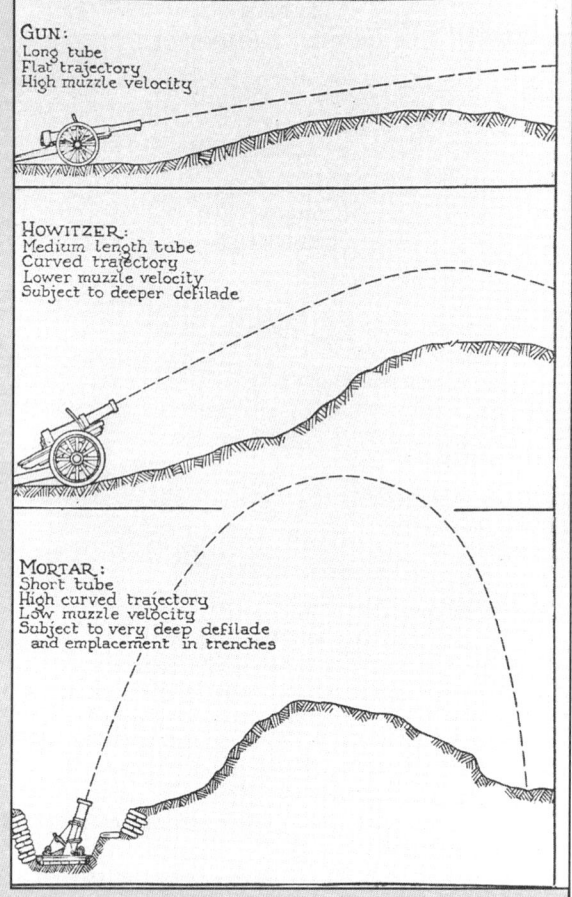

GUN:
Long tube
Flat trajectory
High muzzle velocity

HOWITZER:
Medium length tube
Curved trajectory
Lower muzzle velocity
Subject to deeper defilade

MORTAR:
Short tube
High curved trajectory
Low muzzle velocity
Subject to very deep defilade and emplacement in trenches

Visible in this U.S. Army line drawing are the various differences between a gun, howitzer, and mortar.

Pictured is the American-built copy of a World War I French-designed and -built 155-mm gun called the "Grand Puissance Filloux" (GPF). In U.S. Army service the GPF was designated the M1917. It was the most impressive foreign artillery piece used by American troops in World War I. The gun crew of a GPF could fire a 95-pound high-explosive shell to a maximum range of 12,400 yards. *National Archives*

Artillery Weapons

weapons was the Vickers Mark VI 8-inch howitzer. In American service, the weapon was designated M1917. An American-built copy of the British howitzer was designated M1918. It remained in service until the beginning of World War II as a training weapon.

The French supplied almost 2,000 towed 75-mm guns (designated by the French as 75-mm Mle 1897). This quick-firing, short range, direct-fire weapon was the standard light divisional field artillery weapon of the French army until the start of World War II. American soldiers referred to it simply as the "French 75." When originally developed near the end of the nineteenth century, the "French 75" was a design leap ahead of its foreign counterparts. It brought together a very efficient recoil system with a rapid-action breech design and a carriage that allowed a very high rate of fire. (A breech is a mechanical opening and closing device located on the rear of a barrel that opens for entry of a round and then closes to become a pressure seal for the barrel).

By the beginning of World War I the French 75 had been surpassed in performance by German, Austrian, and British guns of the same general caliber (the caliber of an artillery weapon is the diameter of the bore, not including the depth of the rifling). However, it was the best that the French and Americans had during World War I. During World War I the United States and France were the only major armies not equipped with light field howitzers.

Other French artillery pieces adopted into U.S. Army service during World War I included a fairly large towed howitzer designed by the French firm of Schneider. In U.S. Army service the 155-mm howitzer was designated M1917. It was considered a medium divisional support weapon within the American army and was employed as a longer-range indirect fire supplement to the direct fire French 75.

Another Schneider product that the Americans used was a large towed 155-mm gun, designed by a French lieutenant colonel named Filloux called by the French the Grande Puissance Filloux (GPF), or "Filloux's gun of great power." In U.S. Army service the weapon was designated M1917. American-built copies of the gun with a different breech ring were designated M1918M1. The M1917s were designated M1917A1 when the American-built breech ring was fitted. American soldiers in France sometimes referred to it as the 155-mm rifle. It was considered by its crews as "the best type of heavy field artillery developed during the war," because of its simplicity, wide traverse, efficient recoil system, long-range durability, and "very pleasing appearance."

The Westervelt Board

Embarrassed about the need to depend on foreign artillery pieces, the U.S. Army formed the Westervelt Board in early 1919. (The board was named after its senior ranking officer, Brigadier General William I. Westervelt). It was composed of several officers tasked with defining field artillery for the U.S. Army of the future.

The Westervelt Board interviewed artillery officers from different armies and inspected Allied and enemy artillery weapons and manufacturing plants. When the board finished its survey in May of 1919, it concluded that every

---

Artillery Tactical Classifications

Artillery pieces are classified as either fixed or mobile. Mobile artillery pieces are further subclassified as railway, self-propelled or towed. Weapons are grouped into these classifications in accordance with the characteristics of their carriages, rather than their tubes.

Starting in World War I, the U.S. Army classified all guns and howitzers into light, medium and heavy categories.

Light artillery pieces up to and including 105-mm howitzers are chiefly employed against enemy troops. They are used in the indirect fire role or in close-up combat with the infantry in direct fire. Light pieces are the most mobile of the three weight categories.

The 155-mm howitzer and other medium artillery pieces are used for fire on enemy artillery, dug-in infantry, and targets of considerable resistance. Medium artillery is also used to reinforce the fire of light artillery. Medium artillery pieces generally have greater range and payload than light artillery, but lower mobility.

Heavy artillery pieces such as the 155-mm gun are used for fire missions requiring greater range and destructive power. Heavy artillery pieces generally have poor mobility, and some even require partial disassembly before they can be moved.

Light and medium artillery pieces are generally found at the divisional level. Heavy artillery pieces are normally attached at a much higher level such as corps (which normally consists of two to three divisions) or army level (which may normally consist of two to three corps). Heavy artillery units can be temporarily detached to support divisional level artillery units for specific assignments.

Early production examples of the T30 were designed without armored protection for the highly exposed gun crew, who stood up in the back of the vehicle to service their weapon. Combat experience in the Philippines during late 1941 and early 1942 convinced the Ordnance Department that an armored gun-shield was highly desirable. A number of different types were tried, but eventually a tall boxlike arrangement as seen in this picture was approved for production. *National Archives*

Early production examples of the U.S. Army's 75-mm Pack Howitzer M1 came designed for horse towing. They could also be broken down into six separate components for mounting on the backs of mules for steeper terrain. To keep the weight of the weapon down to facilitate its movement by animal transport, it had a lightweight, perforated box trail supported by wooden spoked wheels. Reflecting a number of production changes, the weapon was later designated the M1A1. *National Archives*

type of gun, howitzer, projectile, gun mount, carriage, and vehicle in use by the army had at least one major flaw. As General Westervelt expressed it: "every item of the hardware of war needed improvement."

The Westervelt Board developed a wish list of "ideal" artillery pieces that would satisfy the army's future needs. Unfortunately, most of the recommendations made by the Board in 1919 were not implemented until the late 1930s, due to a severe reduction in artillery development funding after 1921.

75-mm Pack Howitzer

One of the few Westervelt Board recommendations to be implemented fairly quickly was the new lightweight towed 75-mm howitzer that entered service in 1927 as the Pack Howitzer M1.

The U.S. Army's chief of field artillery was so pleased with the new howitzer that he stated in a 1932 magazine article: "It is a remarkable weapon with a great future."

Despite this praise, only 32 Pack Howitzer M1A1s had been built by the end of June 1940. The army finally stepped up production when World War II was imminent. When the Japanese attacked Pearl Harbor on December 7, 1941, the army had 458 Pack Howitzer M1A1s in service. The genesis of the 75-mm Pack Howitzer M1A1 could be traced back to mountain gun work started by the Ordnance Department before World War I. The Ordnance Department needed something better than the British 2.95-inch howitzer then in use by the U.S. Army. The project was dropped when it became apparent that U.S. Army units sent to fight the Germans in France in 1917 had no use for such a weapon. After World War I, the Westervelt Board decided that a pack howitzer was, "one of the items of artillery in most urgent need of development."

An early attempt to provide a self-propelled chassis for the Pack Howitzer M1A1 resulted in the T30 75-mm Howitzer Motor Carriage. The T30 consisted of a modified M3 armored half-track with a pack howitzer mounted to fire over the front of the vehicle. Patton's tank and armored reconnaissance units used them in the North Africa and Sicily campaigns.

Set up in a dugout protected by sandbags and covered by a camouflage net, the crew of a U.S. Army 75-mm M1A1 pack howitzer prepares for a fire mission. With the widespread introduction of wheeled and tracked vehicles into the U.S. Army in the 1930s, a new split-trail carriage designated the M8 with pneumatic tires was provided for the small howitzer. The weapon fired a 13.76-pound high-explosive round to a maximum range of 9,760 yards. *National Archives*

The general layout of the hull of the M8 75-mm howitzer motor carriage was very similar to the M5 light tank. Because of the open-topped turret of the M8, the Ordnance Department decided to eliminate the overhead hatches for the driver and assistant driver. Two armored hatches in the front hull of the M8 provided direct vision forward for the driver and assistant driver. *National Archives*

The T30 was a temporary solution for the army. Work on a full-tracked mount based on the M5 light tank began in December of 1941. The howitzer was placed in an open-topped, 360-degree rotating armored turret and was operated by two men. Successful testing of the T47 vehicles resulted in a production go-ahead in May of 1942. Production of the M8 75-mm howitzer motor carriage began in September of 1942 and continued through January of 1944. A total of 1,778 M8s were built. M8s saw action with Patton's Third Army between July 1944 and the end of the war in Europe.

105-mm Howitzer

The need for a new American towed 105-mm light divisional howitzer was one of great controversy during most of its developmental history. During World War I, U.S. Army Colonel Charles P. Summerall visited France on a fact-finding mission to

A member of the gun crew of a U.S. Army 105-mm howitzer M2A1 peers over the top of his heavily camouflaged weapon with a pair of binoculars to search out potential targets. The 105-mm howitzer employed a percussion firing mechanism. A firing mechanism is a device located on or in a breech mechanism of a weapon to ignite the primer. The primer in turn ignites the propelling charge of a round of ammunition. *National Archives*

46   **Artillery Weapons**

observe new trends in artillery employment. Summerall (later chief of staff) quickly concluded that the French 75 was ineffective as a divisional support weapon and urged that a 105-mm howitzer be developed as quickly as possible. His superiors ignored his recommendation.

After World War I, the Westervelt Board also suggested it would be wise for the army to push the development of a 105-mm howitzer. The board's recommendation met resistance because of the projected expense of the project. Another problem was the fact that the army still had 4,236 French 75s in the inventory and huge stocks of ammunition for the gun. The army's bean counters saw no reason to replace a perfectly serviceable existing weapon with a yet-to-be-proven new weapon.

Despite this lack of interest in 105-mm howitzers the Ordnance Department drew up specifications and began testing a number of experimental 105-mm howitzers in 1920, with poor results.

The Ordnance Department lack of progress spurred the army's Field Artillery Board to take

Pictured on outside display at the Virginia Museum of Military Vehicles is an example of a U.S. Army 105-mm Howitzer M2A1 mounted on the split-trail Carriage M2A2. First entering production in 1939, the 105-mm howitzer M2A1 would see service almost everywhere the army campaigned in World War II. It fired a 33-pound high-explosive round to a maximum range of 12,500 yards. After World War II, the army changed its designation to the M102. *Michael Green*

The crew of a 105-mm howitzer M2A1 has its weapon at its full elevation of 66 degrees. Above the barrel (also known as the tube) of the howitzer is a counterrecoil mechanism that returns the barrel from its recoiled position to its firing position and holds it there until fired again. A weapon is said to be "in battery" when it is in its firing position. *National Archives*

Chapter Two 47

U.S. Army gunners of a 105-mm M3 howitzer prepare to fire their weapon during the Battle of the Bulge in December 1944. The M3 was nothing more than a 105-mm M2A1 howitzer barrel shortened by 27 inches. It retained the same breech mechanism as its larger cousin. The barrel was mounted on the M3 (later the M3A1) carriage. These carriages were beefed-up versions of the M8 carriage used for the 75-mm howitzer M1A1. *National Archives*

matters into its own hands. The board began testing German 105-mm howitzers captured during World War I. The German equipment performed so well that the Field Artillery Board recommended its adoption for service use. The chief of the Ordnance Department cited a shortage of proper ammunition and the cost of reconditioning 300 German howitzers as reasons for denying the request. Instead, an American 105-mm howitzer design based on the best features of the German weapons would be pushed into development as fast as funding would allow.

A successful 105-mm howitzer was finally developed in 1934 by the Ordnance Department and was given the designation M2. Fourteen M2 prototypes were tested between 1928 and 1933. In 1939, the Ordnance Department ordered 48 slightly modified M2A1 105-mm howitzers.

Despite the clear superiority of the M2A1 over the obsolete French 75, the army's senior leadership still wanted to modernize the older French gun. Congress was so irritated by this action that it tried to eliminate funding for the

The U.S. Army crew of a 105-mm M3 howitzer has just fired its weapon, and the barrel is in its full recoil position. Recoil is the backward movement of tube and connecting parts after firing and is caused by a reaction of the forward motion of the projectile and hot gases. A recoil system is a mechanism designed to absorb the energy of recoil and to avoid violent movement of the carriage. *National Archives*

48   Artillery Weapons

program in 1939. Congress' frustration with the situation is in a report by a Senate subcommittee on appropriation:

"The 75-mm gun is being supplanted in foreign armies with the 105-mm weapon, which has greater range and fires a heavier missile. Our Ordnance Department is developing such a gun and, undoubtedly, will be ready to go into production. If that is to be the weapon of the future, the committee questions the wisdom of continuing to spend large sums on the old 75s."

It was not until June 1940, when France fell to the Germans, that the U.S. Army made a concerted effort to replace the obsolete French 75s with the new M2A1 105-mm howitzer. It took three years for M2A1 105-mm howitzers to replace the last of the French 75s. The M2A1 would become the workhorse of the American field artillery during World War II with 8,536 units built.

The M7 Howitzer Motor Carriage mounted a limited traverse 105-mm M2A1 howitzer slightly to the right of the vehicle's centerline. The weapon had a maximum elevation of 35 degrees. Early production examples of the vehicle could carry 57 rounds. This figure was later increased to 69 rounds by reducing the number of folding seats within the vehicle. *National Archives*

The T19 Howitzer Motor Carriage consisted of a limited traverse 105-mm M2A1 howitzer mounted on the chassis of a modified M3 armored half-track. The weapon itself was placed directly behind the driver's position. The location of the gun mount forced the relocation of the vehicle's fuel tanks to the rear of the vehicle. The 105-mm howitzer had a maximum elevation of 35 degrees. *National Archives*

Chapter Two   49

The M3 105-mm howitzer was a cut-down, short-barreled version of the M2A1. It was ordered by the Army Ground Forces in 1941 to be issued to the new infantry cannon company tactical units that first saw action in 1942 in North Africa. Combat experience soon showed them to be an unwelcome manpower drain on hard-pressed infantry battalions. Since the infantry cannon companies provided no additional capabilities to an infantry division's normal complement of artillery battalions, they were disbanded. The remaining M3s were passed on to the army airborne forces, where they remained in use until the war ended.

The concept of providing infantrymen with towed artillery howitzers was not new. The German army used them with great success during most of World War II. In the U.S. Army, the role of infantry cannon was seen as being better served by the standard 81-mm mortar found in the heavy weapons company of every infantry battalion.

An early attempt to place the M2A1 105-mm howitzer on a self-propelled mount resulted in the production of 324 105-mm howitzer motor carriages, designated T19, in early 1942. The T19 consisted of a modified army M3 armored half-track with the 105-mm howitzer positioned to fire over the front of the vehicle. There was limited traverse for the howitzer. They would perform fairly well for Patton's troops in North Africa and Sicily, until the far superior M7 105-mm howitzer motor carriage superseded them.

The M7 consisted of a 105-mm howitzer placed on the open-topped chassis of an M3 medium tank. The howitzer was positioned to fire over the front of the vehicle, with a provision for only limited traverse. The first model rolled out of the factory in April of 1942. Production of the M7 continued until the end of the war, with a total of 3,490 units fielded.

A second version of the M7 was based on the open-topped chassis of an M4A3 model of the

On the M7 and the later M7B1 an M2 .50-caliber air-cooled machine gun was mounted on the right side of the howitzer, primarily for protection from enemy aircraft. The mount for the machine gun on the M7 protruded slightly above and outside the crew compartment. A crew of six manned the vehicle: commander, driver, gunner, and three ammunition handlers. The driver sat on the lower left-hand side of the howitzer. *National Archives*

Sherman medium tank and was designated M7A1. Like the M7, the 105-mm howitzer mounted on the M7A1 was positioned to fire over the front of the vehicle and had only limited traverse. Production of the M7A1 totaled 826 units, with the last unit being completed in February 1945. The M7 and M7A1 saw action with Patton's troops between July 1944 and the end of the war in Europe.

In a World War II U.S. Army Intelligence report, an American general commented on his division's impressions of the M7:

"We have been in combat 63 days with the M7s and during that time we have had very few weapons out on account of motor trouble. Their extreme mobility has been very useful in the terrain and especially during the Cherbourg campaign and the breakthrough. I like them and the men like them."

To overcome the disadvantage of mounting the 105-mm howitzer on an open-topped chassis with limited traverse, the Ordnance Department decided to place a 105-mm howitzer inside the fully enclosed 360-degree rotating armored turret of the M4 and M4A3 versions of the Sherman medium tank.

A total of 1,641 of the M4 version of the Sherman tank armed with the 105-mm howitzer left the factory between February 1944 and March 1945. Production of the M4A3 version of the Sherman tank, armed with the 105-mm howitzer, began in May 1944 and ended in

Crewmen of a U.S. Army M4A3 medium tank armed with a turret-mounted 105-mm howitzer are removing ammunition from its shipping containers prior to loading their vehicle for its next fire support mission. Two M4 medium tanks mounting the 105-mm howitzer were normally assigned to the headquarters company of U.S. Army armored division battalions. When introduced into service, they replaced the older-generation M8 75-mm howitzer motor carriage. *National Archives*

Chapter Two

June 1945, with a total of 3,039 units completed. Both versions of the Sherman tank mounting the 105-mm howitzer would serve with Patton's troops from July 1944 until the end of the war in Europe.

During the development of the Sherman tank versions armed with the 105-mm howitzer, the Ordnance Department made a decision that a power traverse system for the howitzer-armed turret was unnecessary. Early combat experience, however, proved this decision to be incorrect. As complaints poured in from the field, the Ordnance Department sought to correct the problem by adding a power traverse system to

A very late production model M4A3 medium tank armed with a turret-mounted 105-mm M4 howitzer. The M4 howitzer was a modified M2A1 howitzer with a cut-down breechblock to better fit within the confines of the vehicle's cramped turret. Spotting features to distinguish the howitzer-equipped versions of the M4 series medium tanks from the standard vehicles mounting the 75-mm main gun include a thicker barrel and a different gun mantle. *National Archives*

Artillery Ammunition

The term "artillery ammunition" includes all munitions, except rockets and shotgun shells, used in American weapons of caliber greater than 0.60 inch. It includes complete rounds and their various components. A complete round comprises all the components necessary to fire a weapon once. These components are, in general, the projectile, the fuse, the propelling charge, and the primer.

A projectile is the part that is fired from a weapon by the force of gases produced by the propelling charge. A fuse is a mechanical device used with a projectile to explode it at the time and in the circumstances desired. The propelling charge generally consists of a charge of smokeless powder, with an igniter charger of black powder, assembled in a suitable cartridge case, cloth bag, or both. A primer is the component used to initiate the ignition of a propelling charge. Artillery primers consist essentially of a small quantity of sensitive explosive and a charge of black powder encased in a metal container.

Dependent upon the components for firing and the method of loading into the cannon, complete rounds of artillery ammunition are known as fixed, semifixed, or separate-loading.

Complete rounds are those in which the propelling charge is fixed, or not adjustable, and loaded into the cannon as a unit. These rounds are known as "fixed ammunition." Complete rounds in which provisions are made for adjusting the propelling charge to be fired and which, like fixed ammunition, are loaded into the cannon as a unit, are known as "semifixed ammunition." Complete rounds in which the components—projectile, propelling charge, and primer—are loaded into the cannon separately are known as "separate-loading ammunition."

The French-built 155-mm Howitzer M1917 used by the U.S. Army during World War I, and its American-built copy designated the M1918, were originally designed with wooden spoked wheels for towing by horse teams. As the artillery branch of the U.S. Army began to replace its horse teams with large and powerful trucks in the late 1930s, the old 155-mm howitzers still in service were modernized with pneumatic tires and air brakes to allow high-speed towing. *National Archives*

Pictured is a dramatic nighttime view of a 155-mm Howitzer M1 at the moment of firing. The M1 had a maximum elevation of 63 degrees and could fire a 95-pound high-explosive shell to a maximum range of 20,100 yards. The shell was made of common forged steel and had comparatively thin walls and a large bursting charge of high-explosives. It was used against personnel and material targets. *National Archives*

Seen here in postwar U.S. Army service is a 155-mm Howitzer M1. The large spring-like devices on either side of the barrel are called equilibrators. They help to overcome the unbalanced weight of a large and heavy barrel on its carriage by keeping the barrel in balance at all angles of elevation so that it may be elevated or depressed easily. *National Archives*

new production vehicles. Sadly, none of these modified vehicles reached the field before the war in Europe ended.

155-mm Howitzer

In recommending the development of a new 105-mm light howitzer for divisional use, the Westervelt Board had discounted the need for a divisional 155-mm medium support howitzer. The French Schneider 155-mm M1917 medium howitzer and its postwar American copy, the M1918, had proven unpopular during World War I, due to their heavy weight and resulting poor mobility.

After World War I, General John J. Pershing and others blamed the large-scale use of artillery for the static positional warfare that had developed in Western Europe. To prevent a recurrence, Pershing suggested that the army be organized into smaller, highly mobile divisions with tanks and machine guns. Artillery support was to be provided by guns or howitzers with a caliber of 75-mm or smaller.

The army studied the Westervelt Board and the Pershing recommendations and decided to reinstate the 155-mm howitzer in its infantry divisions in 1929. During the 1920s and 1930s the army began a modernization program for its aging M1917 and M1918 medium 155-mm howitzers to allow high-speed towing by trucks. Simultaneously, Brigadier General Lesley J. McNair began to suggest that the army had placed too much importance on artillery in close support of the infantry. He believed that modern long-range artillery pieces massing their fire together on important targets could be supremely effective on the battlefields of the future. McNair therefore urged that the army's infantry divisions reduce the number of light guns and howitzers and increase the number of medium howitzers.

Field tests conducted by the army in 1937 had again confirmed McNair's belief that the 155-mm howitzer, M1917 and M1918, was still superior to the new prototype 105-mm M2 howitzer, due to its ability to deliver more bang for the buck.

Additional tests in 1938 and information on foreign medium artillery development further pointed to the need for a 155-mm medium howitzer in its infantry divisional structure. A few days after the French-German armistice in June

1940, the army adopted a new infantry division structure with four artillery battalions; three direct support battalions of 105-mm howitzer (54 pieces) and one general support battalion of 155-mm howitzers (12 pieces).

The Ordnance Department had begun work in 1939 on a replacement for the aging M1917 and M1918 155-mm howitzer. That replacement arrived as the M1 155-mm howitzer in early 1942. It featured a new longer barrel as well as a new carriage.

The M1 155-mm howitzer was often referred to by American cannoneers as "the sweetest weapon on the front" due to its outstanding accuracy. By the end of the war American factories had built over 6,000 of the howitzers. They would see heavy use with Patton's troops from July 1944 until the war ended in Europe.

The older M1917 and M1918 155-mm howitzers would soldier on until 1943, when enough of the new M1 155-mm howitzers reached ar-

A U.S. Army 155-mm Howitzer M1 battery prepares for a firing mission in this post-World War II picture. Prior to a firing mission the crew of an M1 lowered a firing jack (pedestal) located under the center axle of the weapon. Once this device was in place, the two wheels were raised. This resulted in a three-point support system for the gun, one point of contact being the firing jack and the other two points being the spades of the trail. This arrangement improved both the stability of the weapon and its accuracy. *National Archives*

Being towed behind a U.S. Army artillery tractor in this early World War II picture is a 155-mm Gun M1. Clearly visible are the four dual front tires that carried the main weight of the gun when towed. Also visible is the two-wheel limber (cart) that supported the trail legs when in the towed position. The M1 could fire a 95-pound high-explosive shell to a maximum range of 25,395 yards. *National Archives*

Chapter Two   55

tillery units in the field. American artillerymen affectionately referred to the old M1917 and M1918 howitzers "as faithful old dogs."

155-mm Gun/8-Inch Howitzer

One of the weapons that received the most praise from artillerymen interviewed after the war by the Westervelt Board was the French-designed heavy 155-mm gun commonly called the GPF. Hence, the Westervelt Board recommended the Ordnance Department develop an improved 155-mm heavy gun. The board urged the development of a self-propelled version, so the Ordnance Department began experimenting with a variety of gun carriages. The program yielded no major results until the summer of 1930, when a revolutionary new split-trail T2 carriage appeared.

The T2 carriage had all-welded construction, and four dual front tires—two new features never seen before on heavy field artillery carriages. The unique wheel arrangement at the front of the carriage carried most of the gun's weight. A two-wheel limber (cart) supported the trail legs and helped to distribute the total weight of the carriage and towing vehicle among many wheels to improve overall mobility. The limber was detached from the carriage when the gun was emplaced for firing. The trails of light and medium artillery pieces were supported by the rear towing pintles of prime mover vehicles and were not equipped with limbers.

The T2 carriage, standardized as the M1 in July of 1940, carried a new 155-mm gun (also designated M1). The new gun had a longer barrel and larger firing chamber than the older M1918 155-mm gun. Due to the funding constraints imposed on the prewar army, only 65 of the new M1 guns had been built before 1941.

Under the cover of a large tree and with the help of a truck-mounted crane, the crew of a U.S. Army 155-mm Gun M1 is about to remove the barrel of its gun for replacement. The barrel sat on top of a support called the cradle. The cradle, which housed the recoil, counterrecoil, and recuperator cylinders, was mounted on antifriction trunnion bearings of the top carriage. The top carriage housed the elevating and traversing mechanisms. *National Archives*

Pictured in its traveling configuration is an 8-inch Howitzer M1. The artillery piece was envisioned from the start as a sister piece to the 155-mm Gun M1 and was intended to use the same carriage mounting with a different barrel. Other than its shorter and thicker barrel, the two artillery pieces looked almost identical from a distance. The 8-inch howitzer could fire a high-explosive round weighing 200 pounds to a maximum range of 18,500 yards. *National Archives*

Production was quickly accelerated after the Japanese attack on Pearl Harbor pulled the United States into World War II.

To most American soldiers, the M1 155-mm gun was known as the Long Tom. The Long Tom first saw action with Patton's troops during the North Africa campaign in early 1943. In that campaign they quickly proved their worth.

By mid-February of 1943, the 24 Long Toms in North Africa had been fired so often with maximum range supercharged rounds that their gun

The U.S. Army crew of a 155-mm Gun M1 is busily deploying the two sections of the weapon's split trail. The trail sections were attached direct to the bottom carriage of the weapon. The bottom carriage supports the top carriage. The bottom carriage is also fitted with component parts of the mechanism used for rotating the top carriage in traverse. *National Archives*

Chapter Two

The first pilot model of the 155-mm Gun Motor Carriage M12 is seen in its original configuration at the U.S. Army Aberdeen Proving Ground in February 1942. The 155-mm gun was carried at the rear of the vehicle on the M4 pedestal mount. To leave room at the rear of the vehicle for installing the gun mount, the engine was moved forward to just behind the driver's and assistant driver's compartment. *National Archives*

The 155-mm gun on the M12 could be elevated to a maximum of 30 degrees, and was made steady for firing by a hydraulically actuated spade at the rear of the vehicle. On-board ammunition storage on the vehicle was limited to only 10 155-mm shells located on the carriage floor. Seating for the four-man gun crew consisted of two seats on the left side of the gun mount and two on the spade when it was in the retracted position for traveling. *National Archives*

tubes (barrels) were beginning to wear out. Captured enemy soldiers were so impressed by the gun's sustained rate of fire (one round per minute or a battery burst rate of four or five rounds per minute) that they asked to be shown what they believed was an automatic-loading artillery gun.

Long Toms also served an important role in Patton's campaigns in both Sicily and Western Europe. In Sicily the Long Toms were so effective that the Germans began to dread the Americans' "mad artillery barrages," which they nicknamed "feuerzauber" or fire magic.

Until a sufficient number of Long Toms reached artillery units in the field, the aging French GPF 155-mm gun and its American-built copy (the M1918A1) were in common use. The army had almost 900 of these weapons in the inventory when the United States entered World War II. The army had modernized the carriages of its 155-mm guns to allow high-speed towing by trucks. Patton's troops used the old 155-mm guns during the early stages of the American invasion of North Africa with excellent results.

When the Westervelt Board recommended the development of a new 155-mm heavy gun and carriage in 1919, it set forth almost identical requirements for the carriage of a new 8-inch howitzer that it also recommended for development. This design feature was in line with the Ordnance Department's policy of pairing a gun with a howitzer of approximately the same caliber on an identical carriage.

The same funding problems that bedeviled the development of artillery pieces generally caused the work on a new 8-inch howitzer to be done in fits and starts during the period between the wars.

Pictured in action during the Korean War is the successor of the M12 Gun Motor Carriage, the M40 Gun Motor Carriage. Instead of the M3 tank chassis the Ordnance Department used various late war M4 series medium tank components and mounted the more powerful 155-mm Gun M1 on the new self-propelled mount. Only the two pilot vehicles made it to Western Europe to see action before World War II ended. *National Archives*

Chapter Two   **59**

During World War I, the American army asked the French firm of Schneider to modify one of its existing designs for a heavy howitzer that could be license-built in the United States. Due to various production problems, only one example of the 240-mm howitzer designated the M1918 was built before the war ended. Construction continued after the war, with 330 units completed, one of which is pictured here in U.S. Army service sometime in the 1930s. It could fire a 345-pound high-explosive shell to a range of 16,400 yards. *National Archives*

The weapon finally became authorized for production in 1940 as the 8-inch Howitzer M1. Yet, none were produced prior to the attack on Pearl Harbor. The first production units did not enter service until 1942. In service they soon acquired sterling reputations for both accuracy and their ability to knock out heavily fortified enemy positions. In March 1945, the addition of a new breech ring resulted in the designation M2. Over 1,000 M1s and M2s were built during the war years.

Self-Propelled 155-mm Gun

As additional Long Toms entered army service in 1943, the older generation of towed 155-mm heavy guns was slowly retired. In June 1941, the chief of ordnance came up with an innovative idea. He suggested mounting some of the remaining cannons on the open-topped chassis of surplus M3 medium tanks. In this configuration they could be employed as very cost-effective self-propelled artillery guns. A prototype designated the T6 Gun Motor Carriage (GMC) began undergoing testing in February of 1942. During a comparison test between the T6 and a towed artillery piece, the T6 moved 6 miles to a new firing position in only 35 minutes. It took the crew of the towed gun over three hours to reach the same firing position.

Despite the positive test results with the T6, the Army Ground Forces could not see a need for such a weapon. They believed that the existing towed guns would fulfill all battlefield needs. On the other hand, the Ordnance Department remained convinced of a future need for a self-propelled 155-mm gun. In March 1942, the T6 was approved for production as the M12 GMC, with 50 vehicles ordered. The quantity was increased to 100 vehicles on August 10, 1942. The first production M12 rolled off the production line in September of 1942.

The Army Ground Forces continued to express little interest in the project and placed some of the M12s into storage while others were assigned to stateside training units. Their interest in the M12 GMC began to grow in late 1943 as plans for the invasion of Western Europe were being formulated. Not long afterward, Army Ground Forces made a decision that resulted in the remanufacture and modernization of 74 of the M12s for possible overseas service. The first M12s arrived in France in July 1944 and were attached to Bradley's First Army and Patton's Third Army.

This extract from Dick Hunnicutt's well-known book on the Sherman tank series and its variants describes the use of the M12 in 1944 and 1945:

"In action in Europe, the M12 fully justified the effort that went into its development. It was particularly effective in supporting the fast-moving columns after the breakout from Normandy. On a number of occasions these self-propelled guns were the only heavy artillery within a day's march of the front, and they successfully performed all of the normal missions for such weapons.

"When the attacking armies came up against the heavy fortifications of the Siegfried Line in the fall of 1944, the M12 proved to be an effective mean for their destruction. Using direct fire at ranges of 1,000 to 2,000 yards the 155-mm shells were deadly to the pillboxes. With concrete piercing fuses, the high-explosive rounds could penetrate up to 7 feet of reinforced concrete. Frequently, only one or two shots was required to cause the pillbox crew to surrender."

Once Army Ground Forces became aware of just how useful the M12 was in the field, it quickly requested additional vehicles. The problem was that the Ordnance Department had exhausted its inventory of M1917, M1917A1, and M1918A1 155-mm guns, and the newer Long Tom was too big to be mounted on a surplus M3 medium tank chassis. Instead, the Long Tom gun was mounted on a new full-tracked chassis designated T43.

The specially designed T43 chassis consisted of late-model Sherman medium tank components. To provide a more stable firing platform as well as more room for the gun crew, the hull of the T43 was wider than that of the M12. Production of the T43 (later standardized as the M40 155-mm GMC) began in February of 1945. By the end of 1945 the army received 418 vehicles. Two early test model M40s saw action during the closing stages of the war, but no production units made it into service before the war in Europe ended.

240-mm Howitzer/ 8-inch Gun

While the Germans were demonstrating the spectacular effectiveness of dive-bombers and tanks in the early years of the war, the army's interest in heavy artillery was almost nonexistent. Army Ground Forces' interest was revived after the fighting in Tunisia (North Africa) in early 1943, when American forces encountered the German 170-mm gun for the first time. The German gun (designated 17-cm K18) easily out-ranged the U.S. Army's Long Tom.

Wheels removed and ready for action, the 240-mm Howitzer M1 was a massive affair that weighed over 30 tons. The trench behind the 27-foot, 7-inch barrel was dug between the trail legs to allow the breech to recoil at its maximum elevation of 65 degrees. Visible midway along the side of the trail leg in the foreground is an outrigger that aided in stabilizing the weapon. At the end of the trail legs can be seen two large flat plates known as floats. Like the outrigger, they were also used to brace a weapon when fired. *National Archives*

Prior to the start of the North African campaign in November 1942, Army Ground Forces had convinced itself that nothing larger than the Long Tom would be needed during the war. Once this shortsighted decision was seen to be in error, the Ordnance Department pulled out all the stops to place larger and more powerful heavy artillery pieces into service. Only heavy artillery could provide sustained, accurately placed fire on a round-the-clock basis regardless of weather conditions.

Reflecting the Army Ground Forces' new outlook on the importance of artillery, General Lesley McNair commented after an inspection trip to North Africa in May 1943:

"Instead of artillery becoming an arm which is tending to fade out of the picture under the pressure of air power or tanks, it is there in the same strength and importance that it had in the [first] World War."

As far back as 1919, the Westervelt Board was fully aware of the important role of heavy artillery in any future war. It had recommended a new 8-inch gun and 240-mm howitzer be developed along with a carriage that would serve both weapons. A French-designed 240-mm howitzer built in the United States after World War I (designated M1918M1) was to serve as a point of departure for the new heavy howitzer. Because of funding shortages, nothing came of the Westervelt Board recommendations until 1939, when World War II started. The Ordnance Department was now given the money needed to get a new 8-inch gun and 240-mm howitzer off the drawing boards and into production.

The howitzer was standardized in the spring of 1943 as the 240-mm Howitzer M1. The 8-inch gun was authorized for production in December 1943 as the 8-inch Gun M1. The great length of the barrels on both weapons prevented the transport of their massive carriages and barrels together in a single towed load, so the carriages and barrels of both weapons were transported separately. Once they arrived on site, a mobile crane assembled the weapons back into firing order.

The 240-mm Howitzer M1 was the first to see action with American troops fighting in Italy in January 1944. Firing alongside 8-inch howitzers, the 240-mm howitzer proved an ideal weapon for use in the mountainous terrain of Italy for delivery of explosives to targets on the opposite sides of mountains. Because the maximum range on the 240-mm howitzer was slightly less than the 155-mm Long Tom, the U.S. Army units in Italy needed the longer-ranged 8-inch gun to compete with the German 172.5-mm guns.

The introduction of the 8-inch gun into field units in Italy was delayed because of various problems with the weapon's carriage. Original plans called for the same carriage to serve both the heavy howitzer and the gun. Unfortunately, the carriage in use with the 240-mm howitzer could not accommodate the extra 10 degrees of

1 A 240-mm Howitzer M1 could fire a 360-pound high-explosive shell to a maximum range of 25,225 yards. In this World War II picture, a U.S. Army gun crew of a 240-mm howitzer has a shell on a loading trough. In the lower right corner can be seen the head of a loading rammer that will be used to push the shell into the firing chamber of the weapon. *National Archives*

2 The 240-mm Howitzer M1 fired separate-loading ammunition. This meant that after the shell was rammed home, a propelling charge contained within a cylindrical silk cloth bag, as seen in this picture, was loaded behind it. The amount of propelling charge within the silk cloth bag could be varied depending on the distance to a target. The farther away the target, the more propellant added to the propelling charge. *National Archives*

elevation, so the carriage was modified. Once this problem was solved, the 8-inch guns were shipped to Italy and performed their first firing mission in May 1944. They soon eliminated the threat from the German long-range guns.

After D-Day (June 6, 1944), American military units fighting in Italy lost their priority for equipment. By November 1944, none of the 8-inch guns or 240-mm howitzers remained in Italy; all were in Western Europe.

When the U.S. Army's massive breakout attempt from Normandy (code-named Operation Cobra) was launched in July of 1944, the heavy 8-inch guns and 240-mm howitzers that had been transplanted from Italy played an important role in subduing the German defenses. Once General Omar Bradley's First Army attained the initial breakthrough of the German lines, Patton's Third Army entered the battle. Within a span of a few weeks Patton's troops routed the German forces and were racing across France toward the Germany border. Dur-

3 Two American soldiers are straining to close the breechblock of a 240-mm Howitzer M1. A breechblock is the principal part of the breech mechanism and is essentially a large heavy steel piece, which accurately closes or covers the back end of the barrel. Various safety devices are found on the breech mechanism, such as levers or latches that function automatically to prevent firing the weapon before the breech mechanism is fully closed. *National Archives*

4 An American soldier stands ready to yank on a lanyard connected to a firing mechanism that will fire the 240-mm Howitzer M1 seen in the picture. Once the lanyard was pulled, it cocked and released an inertia-operating firing hammer, which struck a heavy firing pin, which in turned struck a primer. A primer is used to initiate the ignition of a propelling charge. *National Archives*

Chapter Two   **63**

Due to the length and weight of the 240-mm Howitzer M1 (as well as the 8-inch Gun M1) it was necessary to remove the barrel of the weapon from its carriage when transported. The barrel and carriage were each placed on their own separate six-wheeled transport wagon. Pictured is a turretless M3 series medium tank towing a 240-mm howitzer barrel. *National Archives*

American soldiers using a 20-ton truck-mounted crane are pictured lowering the heavy barrel of an 8-inch Gun M1 onto its carriage. Since the 240-mm Howitzer M1 and the 8-inch Gun M1 used the same carriage, the only outward difference between the two weapons was the longer and thinner barrel of the 8-inch gun. The 240-mm howitzer barrel was roughly 27 feet long versus the 34-foot long barrel of the 8-inch gun. *National Archives*

ing this period, there was little requirement for either the 8-inch gun or 240-mm howitzer. This would change as the American armies in Europe (particularly Patton's Third Army) outran their supply lines and could advance no farther. To provide enough trucks to bring supplies forward to the American First and Third Armies during the supply crunch of August and September 1944, many heavy artillery units were stripped of their organic wheeled transport.

As German defenses stiffened in the autumn of 1944, and as winter started to set in, the American ground attack aircraft, which had played such a key role in Patton's race across France, was grounded. Without consistent air support and facing shortages of fuel, ammunition, and other critical supplies, Patton's troops found themselves fighting a type of positional warfare practiced during World War I. The 8-inch guns and 240-mm howitzers were brought forward to deal with heavily fortified German defensive positions.

Between October and November 1944, the old forts that guarded the approaches to the

German-occupied City of Metz in eastern France became the main targets for Patton's Third Army. To the surprise of American artillerymen, the forts proved impervious to the fire of American 240-mm howitzers and to air bombardment. In contrast, the German army had anticipated such defenses and had developed heavy siege-type artillery for destroying thick-walled concrete forts. The Germans were eventually starved out of the forts around Metz; the Americans never destroyed them.

After the Battle of the Bulge (December 1944–January 1945) the need for heavy artillery pieces like the 8-inch gun and the 240-mm howitzer essentially ceased in the Third Army as the advance into Germany picked up speed and the German military began to disintegrate.

Mortars

The advantages of mortars include great tactical mobility, a high rate of fire, a very high trajectory, and adaptability to a variety of terrain conditions. Like all the major armies involved in World War II, the U.S. Army Ground Forces made extensive use of mortars. The two main types employed by the American infantry were the 60-mm and 81-mm mortars. Both types were based on foreign designs.

The mortar also has some disadvantages. Due to the very low muzzle velocity of the finned bombs and their high trajectory, high winds can reduce accuracy to unacceptable levels. In calm weather, however, excellent precision can be attained with mortars. Another disadvantage is the difficulty of maintaining a supply of ammunition. Patton noted this problem in his General Orders issued to the Third Army on March 6, 1944:

"Mortars use great quantities of ammunition. The 81-mm will fire 800 rounds and a 60-mm 500 rounds in 24 hours. To provide this ammunition, transport of all kinds must be utilized, and infantry riflemen in the vicinity of the mortars should each carry one round, which they can dump at a predesignated spot on going into the fire fight. When not on the move, all

Crewmen of an 8-inch Gun M1 have set up a number of projectiles prior to beginning a firing mission. The weapon fired a 240-pound projectile to a maximum range of 33,500 yards. The roughened grooves near the base of the projectiles pictured are called rotating bands. They are made of soft metal and engage the rifling inside the barrel of the gun when the weapon is fired to impart spin to the projectile. *National Archives*

Chapter Two   65

mortars, machine guns, and antitank guns of the infantry must be emplaced to fire."

60-mm and 81-mm Mortars

The U.S. Army's 81-mm mortar program began after World War I, when the French firm of Brandt developed a series of advanced mortar designs based on an older World War I British mortar known as the "Stokes." The Stokes was developed in response to the German army fielding of a crude but effective mortar known as the Minenwerfer in 1914.

During World War I the U.S. Army fielded 1,000 of the Stokes mortar. After World War I the Stokes became the U.S. Army's standard mortar and was designated the Mortar, Trench 3-inch, Mark I and Mark 1A2.

In 1937, the Ordnance Department bought four Stokes mortars that had been improved by the French. They were designated T4 for testing purposes. After successfully passing all tests, the T4 became the 81-mm Mortar M1. Large-scale production of the mortar began in late 1939 or early 1940. It would serve ably throughout World War II in both infantry and armored divisions on all fronts.

In the late 1930s when the U.S. Army decided to develop a standardized armored half-track for its new mechanized units, a self-propelled mortar carrier was proposed. The idea was accepted as being sound and resulted in the fielding of the 81-mm Mortar Carrier M4 in 1942.

Both versions of the vehicle fired the 81-mm mortar over the rear of the armored half-track. This

An American soldier in France is preparing to drop a shell down the barrel of his British-designed Stokes mortar during World War I. Unlike the streamlined and finned mortar bombs used during World War II, the Stokes mortar fired a cylindrical shell without fins. This led to a very erratic flight path and greatly affected the weapon's accuracy. National Archives

mistake was quickly corrected in the final version, on which the mortar was fired over the front of the vehicle. This version of the mortar-carrying armored half-track was designated M21. Production of all versions totaled roughly 1,300 vehicles.

Combat experience with the 81-mm mortar was both positive and negative among American soldiers. A mortar platoon leader in Western Europe commented in a March 1945 report:

"It is my opinion that our own 81-mm mortar is as good as the German 81-mm mortar for infantry work. But in regards to its being used for armor support, I firmly believe that the German 120-mm mortar would fill the bill a great deal better. It is also my suggestion that the mortars be mounted in a more heavily armored vehicle than a half-track. The preference would be a light tank, or medium tank chassis with the gun mounted in such a way as to give it 360-degree traverse."

At the same time the army was testing the Brandt 81-mm mortar, the Ordnance Department bought eight 60-mm mortars from the same firm along with their production drawings. Like the 81-mm mortar, the 60-mm passed all its tests with flying colors and was quickly adopted into service. Minor design changes to ease manufacture distinguished the French version (designated M1) and the American version of the mortar (designated M2).

The first M2 production contract was awarded in early 1940. As the demand for the 60-mm mortar grew before and during the war, other companies were brought in to assist in building the weapon. Production of the 60-mm mortar totaled 50,000 units by the end of the war.

4.2-inch Mortar

The largest and most powerful mortar to see widespread service in the U.S. Army during World War II was a 4.2-inch rifled mortar that first entered production in the 1920s. Like other mortars later adopted into U.S. Army service, the 4.2-inch mortar was based on an improved version of the British Stokes mortar.

Unlike the U.S. Army's 60-mm and 81-mm infantry mortars, the 4.2-inch mortar belonged to the U.S. Army's Chemical Warfare Service (CWS) and was officially designated the 4.2-inch Chemical Mortar. Originally designed to fire

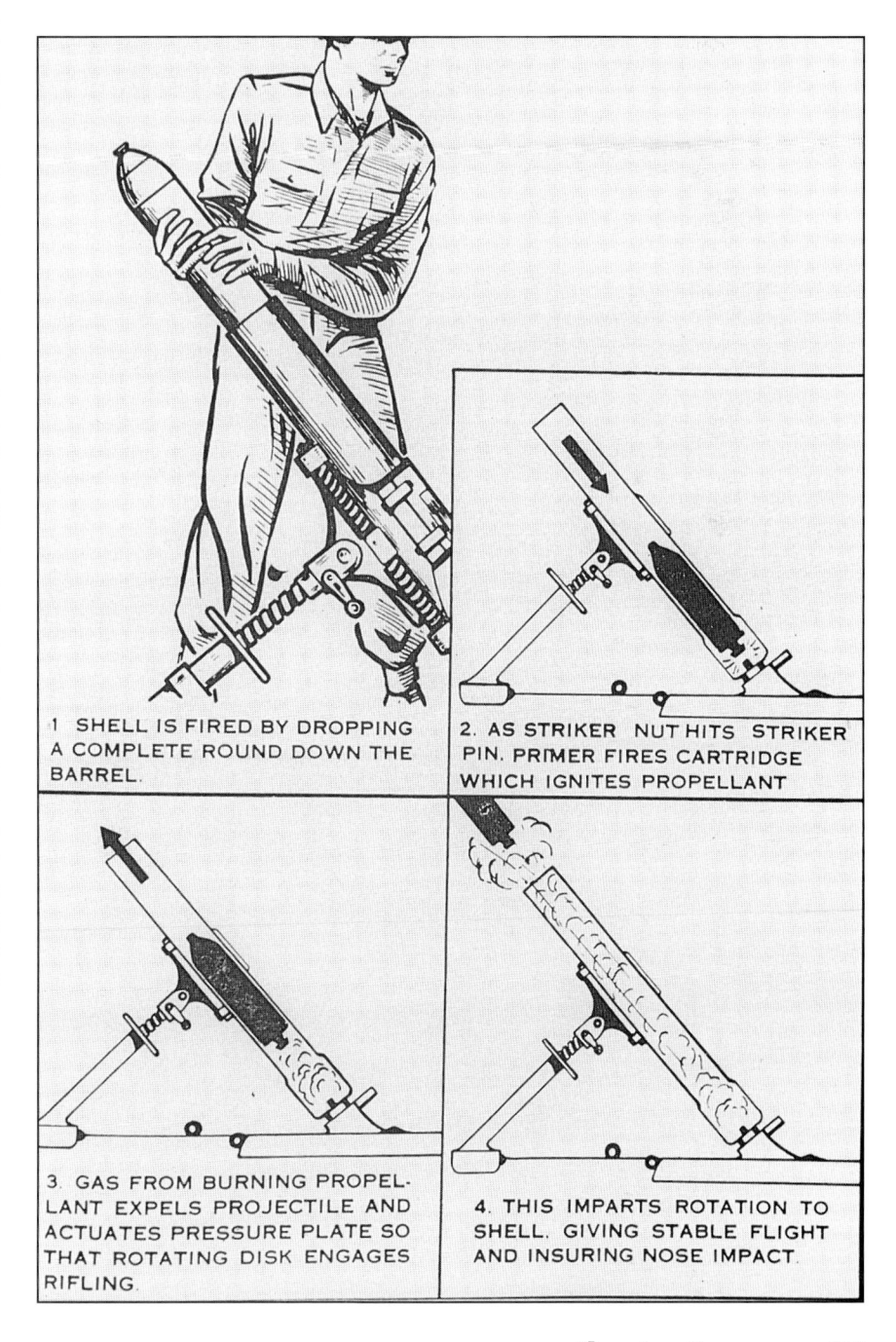

This step-by-step diagram illustrates the mechanics of firing a motor round.

Chapter Two 67

A well-trained crew of a 60-mm M1 Mortar could fire a maximum of 30 rounds per minute for a very brief time. The sustained rate of fire averaged about 18 rounds per minute. The complete mortar with base plate and bipod weighed in at 45.2 pounds. In certain tactical situations, in which targets are very close, the 60-mm mortar could be used by one man in the direct fire role by removing the bipod and substituting a much smaller base plate. *National Archives*

poison gas or smoke shells, the mortar could fire a very effective high-explosive shell, and it became extremely popular with American soldiers late in the war.

The ability of the 4.2-inch chemical mortar to fire high-explosive shells was almost an after thought. Fortunately, General Porter, Chief of the CWS, saw a need for a medium-range infantry support mortar in the early 1930s.

By 1934 the CWS was testing new high-explosive shells, which it fought hard to have standardized into service. Porter wanted to make the firing of such a shell a major mission of the chemical mortar battalions. Permission was finally given in 1942. The difficulty that followed was convincing the ground commanders to include 4.2-inch mortar battalions in their commands.

The outstanding effectiveness of the 4.2-inch chemical mortar battalions serving in Patton's Seventh Army in Sicily in July 1943 soon

A crew of an American 81-mm M1 Mortar takes a break between firing missions to check coordinates on its maps. The 81-mm M1 mortar was a smoothbore, muzzle-loading, high angle-of-fire weapon, capable of a high degree of accuracy. It consisted of three main components seen in this picture: the barrel, the bipod, and the base plate. The total weight of the assembled mortar was 115 pounds. *National Archives*

68   Artillery Weapons

An American soldier is looking through an M4 Sight on his 81-mm M1 Mortar. After the gunner sets the sights, he lays the mortar. Laying the mortar is putting the proper angle of elevation on the barrel and sighting the mortar in the proper direction. The 81-mm mortar was an excellent weapon for firing on area targets, such as troops in the open and in assembly areas. It fired a 6.87-pound shell to a maximum range of 3,290 yards. *National Archives*

convinced the fighting troops that they were a worthy addition to the inventory. Among the comments made by officers whose units were supported in combat by 4.2-inch mortars were "the equivalent of real artillery," which the chemical mortar was not, and "the most effective single weapon used in support of infantry," a statement whereto it had fair claim.

An example of the effectiveness of the 4.2-inch chemical mortar in the type of engagement that so impressed American soldiers is recounted in this extract from the official U.S. Army history of World War II:

"Actually, the chemical mortars had the necessary accuracy to engage targets as small as a tracked vehicle. Just before dawn on one of the early days of the Sicily campaign, a temporarily disabled German tank began harassing an infantry position with automatic fire as the crew

Pictured are two members of the five-man crew of a 60-mm M1 Mortar. The weapon was a smoothbore, muzzle-loading, high-angle-of-fire weapon. In U.S. Army service during World War II it was used to provide close support to a rifle company in the attack and defense by placing mortar fire on small area targets, such as crew-served weapons and small groups of personnel. It fired a three-pound shell a maximum range of 1,985 yards. *National Archives*

Chapter Two   **69**

made repairs. Asked for help by the infantry company, a 2d Chemical Battalion company commander called for one sensing round and then a volley of eight. The tank was silenced. Daylight examination of the tank found all mortar rounds within an area of 15 yards in diameter, with one of them down the open turret of the vehicle."

As a component of Patton's Third Army in Western Europe in 1944 and 1945, the 4.2-inch chemical mortars again proved their worth in combat. On many occasions the mortar battalions could hold off enemy attacks for long periods, avoiding the need for regular divisional artillery units to go into action. Due to their size and weight, the 4.2-inch chemical mortar battalions served best when the tactical situation was static. In the Third Army's rapid advance across France between July and October 1944 and other fast-moving situations, the value of the mortars decreased.

Mounted on the top of a U.S. Army M4A3 medium tank is the T34 Rocket Launcher. It consisted of 90 long plastic tubes, each of which contained a 4.5-inch rocket. The rockets could be fired electrically either in single or salvo fire. The launcher was controlled in azimuth and elevation with the same controls as those used for the main armament mounted in the tank turret. *National Archives*

Shown at the moment of firing is a 4.2-inch M2 Mortar (nicknamed the four-deuce). It was a rifled, muzzle-loading weapon firing 32-pound high-explosive shells to a maximum range of 4,400 yards. The assembled mortar weighed in at a hefty 333-pounds and was serviced by a crew of eight men. To steady the 4.2-inch mortar pictured, the crew has piled sandbags on top of the weapon's base plate. *National Archives*

A crewman of a 4.2-inch M2 Mortar is turning the elevating wheel on his weapon. The 4.2-inch mortar was normally fired as a battery consisting of a number of platoon units (four mortars in a platoon). To increase the effectiveness of the weapon, the fire of an entire company of mortars could be concentrated on a single target. In such cases, the fire of the mortars was concentrated by a fire direction center and was adjusted on targets by forward observers, who accompanied front line rifle units. *National Archives*

Chapter Three

Armored Fighting Vehicles

In World War I (1914-1918) not a single American-designed and built tank saw combat. U.S. Army tank units in Europe were issued foreign-built vehicles. The French supplied the U.S. Army with the Renault FT-17 light tank, a small two-man vehicle weighing six tons. The FT-17 was armed with either an 8-mm machine gun or a short-barreled 37-mm gun. A 39-horsepower, four-cylinder gasoline engine powered the tank, giving it a top speed of 5 miles per hour. With a 24-gallon fuel tank, the vehicle had a maximum range of 22 miles.

World War I U.S. Army armored units also employed the British Mark V heavy tank. With an odd rhomboidal shape and circumferential tracks, the 32-ton vehicle was primarily designed to cross enemy trenches. It had an eight-man crew and was fitted with two 57-mm guns located in small compartments on either side of the hull. The Mark V tank was also fitted with up to six machine guns. It had a top speed of 5 miles per hour and had a maximum range of 25 miles.

The U.S. government obtained production rights for modified versions of the French light tank and the British heavy tank. A handful of American-built copies of the French light tanks reached Europe but saw no combat action. The American-built copy of the British heavy tank was still in the prototype stage when the war ended.

Based on its World War I combat experience, the army infantry branch concluded that medium tanks were optimal for the battlefield of the future. By the mid-1920s the infantry branch had lost interest in the development of medium tanks and turned instead to the development of highly mobile light tanks.

In 1927, the infantry branch tested a prototype light tank known as the T1. Finally, in 1936 after a long series of false starts, it fielded the M2A1 light tank, armed with two machine guns. The M2A1 light tank had a four-man crew and featured an air-cooled Continental radial engine, front-mounted transmission, vertical volute spring suspension (VVSS) system, and rubber block tracks mounted on a steel frame. These features and others resulted in a very dependable vehicle that laid the groundwork for the design of future generations of American tanks.

Between 1919 and the late 1930s, the most numerous armored fighting vehicle in the U.S. Army inventory was the M1917 light tank, as pictured on display at the First Infantry Division Museum. Over 900 were built in American factories in 1918. The M1917 was copied from a French-designed light tank known as the FT-17, which first appeared in service during World War I. *Michael Green*

M3 and M5 Light Tanks

Observations of tank battles in Europe during 1939 and 1940 led the U.S. Army Ordnance Department to develop an improved version of the M2A4. The turret-mounted 37-mm gun was retained, but the turret armor-protection was

U.S. Army Ordnance Department Nomenclature

In the U.S. Army system of weapon designations, the letter "T" meant test number. Once an item of equipment was approved for production (standardized), a vehicle received an "M" or model number. The M number did not necessarily correspond with the T number. A number denoting its order of seniority in the Ordnance Department system followed all T and M weapon designations. An example of this numbering system can be seen with the army's prewar and wartime medium tanks, starting with the M2 in 1939, the M3 in 1940, and finally the M4 in 1941. The letter "A" following the number designation represented interior or exterior improvements and modifications to a piece of equipment. A number after the "A" denoted the order of seniority of the improvement or modification; i.e., the M4A3 medium tank. The letter "E" denoted major external improvements to a particular piece of equipment. A number after the "E" denoted the order of seniority of the external improvements, e.g., the specially modified M4A3E2 assault tank.

increased. The suspension system was upgraded to carry the added weight of the extra armor. These changes and others resulted in a new designation of M3, which entered production in March 1940.

During the production of the M3 a number of improvements were incorporated, including a change from riveted to welded turret and hull construction. This change was aimed mainly at saving weight but also eliminated the danger of rivet heads becoming projectiles inside the vehicle if high-velocity antitank rounds hit it. The final M3 variant was the M3A3, of which production started in early 1943.

Due to a continuing shortage of Continental air-cooled radial engines, the Ordnance Department was very receptive to a suggestion by the Cadillac Division of the General Motors Corporation to mount two Cadillac car engines along with its Hydra-Matic transmission in an M3. Tests soon proved the viability of the concept and production began of a modified M3A3 designated the M5 in April 1942.

To make room for the additional engine, the M5's rear engine compartment was enlarged. A sloped front hull armor plate was added to provide more room for the driver and assistant driver. This feature also was incorporated into the production line of the M3A3. An improved turret, developed originally for the M3A3, was

The M2A3 light tank was a progressively improved version of the M2A1 light tank, which appeared in U.S. Army service in 1936. The M2A3 had two turrets, each armed with a machine gun. Due to the twin-turret designs of the M2A2 and M2A3 light tanks, they were nicknamed the "Mae West" after the well-endowed movie actress of the time. *National Archives*

In 1938, at the request of the chief of the infantry branch, a single example of the M2A3 light tank was taken from the production line to be fitted with heavier armor and more powerful armament. This modified vehicle, adopted and designated the M2A4, had a single turret armed with a 37-mm gun and a coaxial .30-caliber machine gun. The M2A4 tanks pictured are being directed onto railroad flatcars for shipment to a training area. *National Archives*

Chapter Three   73

Service use of the M2A4 light tank highlighted the need for numerous improvements in the vehicle's design. The design of an improved light tank, designated the M3, was authorized in July 1940. Production began in March 1941 and continued until October 1942. Progressively improved versions were designated the M3A1 and M3A3. The restored gasoline-powered M3 series light tank pictured belongs to the Virginia Museum of Military Vehicles. *Michael Green*

also fitted to the M5. The new turret and other improvements resulted in the designation M5A1. The M5 and M5A1 eventually replaced the various versions of the M3, to become the most numerous light tanks in the U.S. Army inventory during World War II.

Until the U.S. Army saw its first combat action against the German army, in North Africa in early 1943, light tanks were the centerpiece of the army's armored divisions. Sadly the U.S. Army's faith in light tanks soon disappeared when German tank and antitank guns turned them into deathtraps. At the end of the campaign in North Africa, General Omar Bradley stated: "Operations in Tunisia have indicated that the use of the light tank M5 in other than reconnaissance missions resulted in excessive losses." Other senior army officers involved in the North Africa campaign, including Patton, concurred with Bradley.

Based on the painful lessons learned in North Africa, the U.S. Army Ground Forces began to replace the light tanks with medium tanks. The remaining light tanks were relegated

Pictured during one of the large-scale training exercises conducted in the southern United States prior to America's entry into World War II is a U.S. Army M2A4 light tank. Production of the vehicle, powered by an air-cooled radial gasoline engine, began in May 1940 and continued until March 1941, with 365 units completed. The army used the M2A4 only for training purposes. *National Archives*

74 **Armored Fighting Vehicles**

to secondary duties. Most American tankers would have preferred complete retirement of the dreaded light tanks.

In a World War II report an army officer described the role of light tanks in his tank battalion:

"The light tank is being used for working with infantry. We subject it to direct fire just as little as we can, for it is realized that the armor will not turn the German fire or the 37-mm gun damage the German tanks or SP [self-propelled] guns."

A very lucky U.S. Army staff sergeant who commanded an M5A1 in Western Europe described a combat engagement with a German Panther tank:

"While attacking Weslen, I had my gunner fire two rounds of 37-mm AP [armor piercing] at a Mark V tank at a range of 150 yards. The rounds hit below the right sponson and above the top of the track. The Mark V tank fired three shots back and withdrew to a new position, apparently unharmed. It is my conclusion that there is no role in this war that the light tank M5A1 is capable of handling."

The M5 series light tanks, much like their predecessors, had a four-man crew with the vehicle commander and gunner in the turret and the driver and assistant driver in the front hull. The codriver also operated the flexible .30-caliber bow machine gun. The busiest man on the light tank crew was the vehicle commander. He had to direct the vehicle in combat, load the main gun, and work the turret radio. *National Archives*

The M24 was hampered in combat by its very thin armor protection, with only an inch of armor on the front hull. The gun shield, typically the most heavily armored spot on tanks, was only 1 1/2 inches thick. A crew of five manned the M24. When only four men were available, the assistant driver took over the role of loader for the 75-mm main gun. The M24 pictured is on display at the First Infantry Division museum, located in the outskirts of Chicago. *Michael Green*

Chapter Three   **75**

The M24 light tank was powered by two eight-cylinder, liquid-cooled Cadillac-built gasoline engines giving the vehicle a top speed of 35 miles per hour. The vehicle rode into battle on a torsion bar suspension system with individually sprung dual road wheels, which are evident in this picture of an M24 light tank, belonging to the Virginia Museum of Military Vehicles. *Michael Green*

Obsolete before it could be built in large numbers, the M2A1 medium tank was a design dead end. The Army did allow the builder to complete 94 examples of the vehicle to fulfill its need for training vehicles. No M2A1 tanks ever saw combat. The M2A1 tanks pictured are taking part in a prewar training exercise in the United States. *National Archives*

A New Light Tank Appears

In response to the failure of M3 and M5 light tanks, the Ordnance Department began development of a new light tank specifically for flank security and exploitation. The first result of the Ordnance Department's efforts was the T7. The T7 grew so much in weight during development that it was reclassified as a medium tank. Since the army already had enough medium tanks, a production run of 3,000 M7s was canceled in February 1943.

With the failure of the M7 light tank project, the Ordnance Department went back to the drawing board to develop requirements for another light tank. Cadillac won the competition to design the new tank, which was to combine the best features of their M5 and M5A1 with lessons learned from earlier efforts. Cadillac's effort resulted in the creation of two pilot vehicles designated T24. The T24 was the first ground vehicle to incorporate the lightweight M6 75-mm gun, which had been designed for mounting inside an antishipping version of the B-25 Mitchell medium bomber.

The two T24 pilot vehicles were so successful in tests that the Ordnance Department authorized production of 1,000 vehicles, now designated the M24 "Chaffee." The order was soon raised to 5,000 vehicles. Production of the 18-ton M24 began in March 1944 by both Cadillac and the Massey-Harris Company. The firms produced a total of 4,371 M24s and its variants before war's end.

The first M24s that arrived in Western Europe in December 1944 were well received by American tankers, since they were such a big improvement over the M3 and M5. In a World War

II report, an army officer described a combat engagement involving M24s and German tanks:

"I commanded a company composed of eight M5 and eight M24 light tanks. In our only clash with armor, one of my M24s engaged a German Mark IV frontally at 200 yards. The M24 got off the first rounds, hitting the Mark IV on the front and ricocheting off. This apparently stunned the crew, since we were able to fire a second round before the German tank fired. The second round set the Mark IV on fire. Later examination showed that the first round struck the heaviest front armor and pushed it in about two inches, but did not penetrate. The second round hit a little higher, near the driver's hatch, and did penetrate."

The excitement among American tankers in Western Europe over the arrival of the M24 was tempered by the fact that the vehicle was still underarmored and undergunned compared to most of the German tanks at that time. As a result, most M24s were restricted to escorting armored infantry half-tracks into battle and other lesser duties.

In his general orders of May 1944 Patton explained how he would use light tanks in combat:

"When light tanks are engaging heavier tanks, they must attack by a section, or preferably a platoon. If they will do this, and so operate as to close the ranges to less than 400 yards, they are invariably victorious and at small loss. This close range can be obtained by feigned retreat and ambush or by effective use of the ground."

M3 Medium Tank

The German prewar Mark IV medium tank, originally armed with a 75-mm howitzer, had a

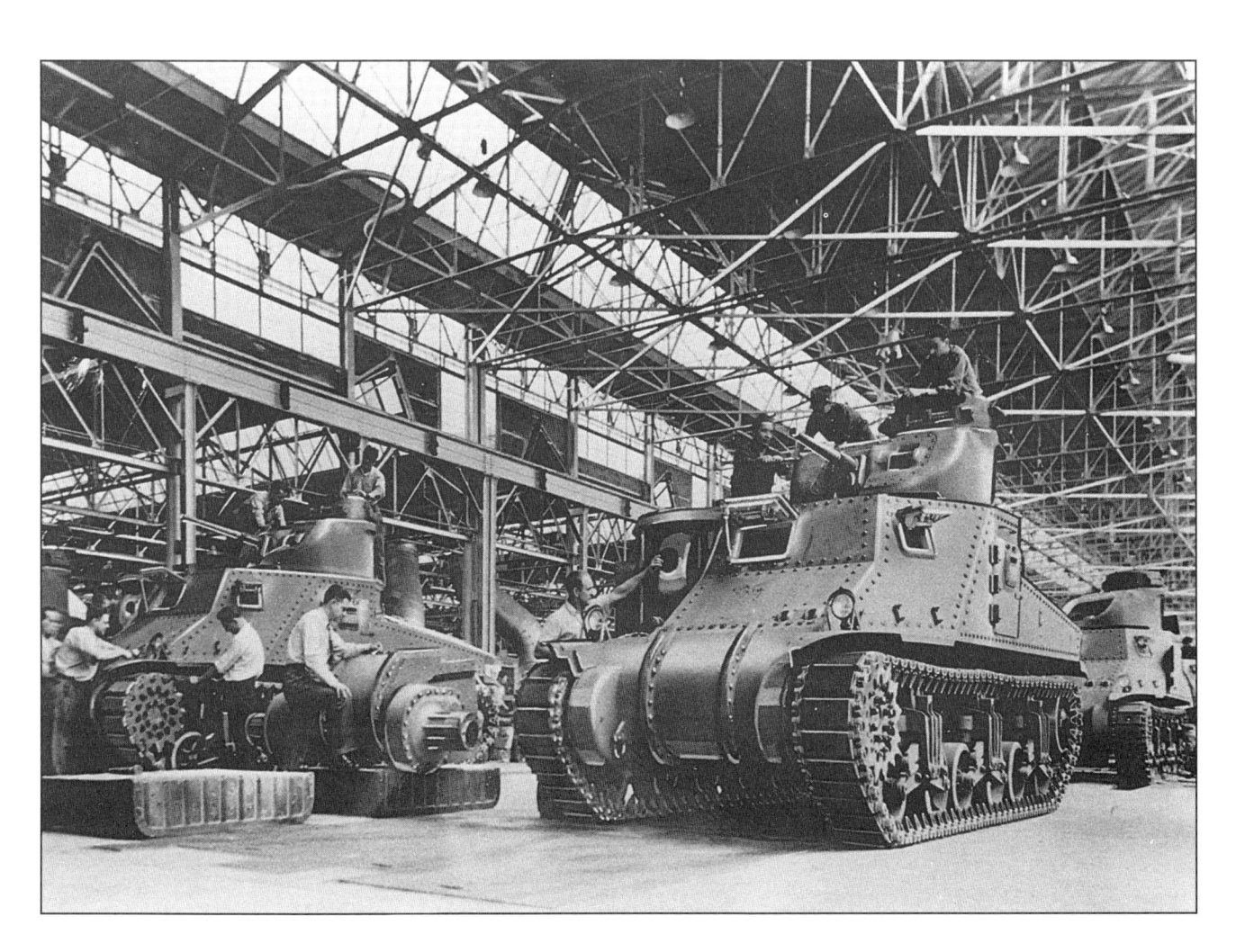

This obviously staged photograph shows a number of M3 medium tanks on the assembly line at the Detroit Tank Arsenal being looked over by Chrysler employees in late 1941. The riveted armored superstructure on these early M3s proved to be a design weakness. When enemy projectiles struck the rivets, they tended to fracture and flew around the within the vehicle causing unnecessary crew losses. *National Archives*

Chapter Three   77

dramatic effect on future American tank design. Prior to the German invasions of Poland (September 1939) and France (May 1940), the U.S. Army and the Ordnance Department had spent most of their time and limited funds developing light tanks armed primarily with machine guns. The U.S. Army had recommended development of the T5 medium tank in late 1936, but their priorities favored light tanks.

The T5 was essentially an enlarged version of the M3 light tank with more firepower and armor protection than other American tanks then in service. The T5 shared many components with the M3. In early 1939 a number of T5 prototypes were tested with different arrangements of main guns and machine guns. The configuration of the T5 was standardized in late 1939 and was designated M2. An improved M2A1 configuration appeared soon afterward. Both configurations were armed with a 37-mm antitank gun and six machine guns.

On August 15, 1940, the U.S. Army awarded a contract to Chrysler Corporation for the production of 1,000 M2A1 medium tanks. They were to be built at a rate of 100 tanks per month. Simultaneously, reports from Europe convinced the army that the M2A1 was already obsolete, and the order was canceled on August 28, 1940. Since Chrysler was already gearing up to produce tanks, the contract was changed to 1,000 of the yet-to-be-designed M3 medium tanks. The M3 was to have thicker armor than the M2A1 and would carry a 75-mm main gun.

However, Chrysler was not ready to build a large turret mounting a 75-mm gun, so a hull-mounted 75-mm gun configuration was used for the M3. The Ordnance Department had already developed an experimental design based on the T5 (the T5E2) that mounted a 75-mm howitzer at the right front of the vehicle. Tests confirmed that this setup was practical for tank installation. The final M3 design was approved in February of

The M3 medium tank weighed about 30 tons fully loaded and had a crew of five men. Armor thickness on the front of the vehicle's hull and turret was 2 inches, with decreasing amounts of thickness on the sides and rear of the tank. The beautifully restored M3 shown belongs to the Virginia Museum of Military Vehicles. It is a late production example, as evident by the lack of the armored side door that is found on earlier production examples. *Michael Green*

78   **Armored Fighting Vehicles**

Unhappy with the poor level of protection offered by riveted steel armor plates, the Army began looking at the possibility of casting the entire upper superstructure of the M3 medium tanks in one piece. Early tests proved the validity of the concept, which resulted in the production of the M3A1 version as pictured. A welded-hull version of the M3 powered by two diesel engines was also built. It was designated as the M3A3, but did not see action with the U.S. Army during World War II. *National Archives*

1941. By August 1941 full-scale production had begun. The tank featured an M2 75-mm gun in a limited-traverse mount (30 degrees right or left) at the right front of the hull. The limited traverse of the M3's main gun was a severe disadvantage during engagements with enemy tanks featuring full-rotation turrets.

Additional armament on the M3 consisted of a 37-mm gun mounted in a small turret on top of the hull superstructure. The riveted superstructure was built of cast and welded steel plates. A later production model featured a cast hull. Secondary armament consisted of four .30-caliber machine guns.

M4 Medium Tank

The first generation of M4 medium tanks (hereafter referred to as the "Sherman," its official British army nickname) were armed with a 75-mm main gun in a 360-degree rotating turret. They proved to be a big improvement over the limited traverse 75-mm main gun found on the M3 medium tanks. Various versions of the Sherman formed the mainstay of the U.S. Army's 16 armored divisions and 65 independent tank battalions during the war years.

American factories produced almost 50,000 Shermans between 1942 and 1945. Many were supplied to America's wartime military allies, including Great Britain, France, and the Soviet Union. Six different first-generation versions of the Sherman were built: the M4, M4A1, M4A2, M4A3, M4A4, and the M4A6. The U.S. Army employed three versions in combat: the M4, M4A1, and the M4A3. The M4A1 version first rolled off the assembly line in February 1942, to be followed by the M4A3 version in June 1942 and the M4 version in July 1942.

The typical first generation Sherman averaged about 35 tons in weight when fully loaded with fuel and ammunition. It rode into battle on the vertical volute spring suspension (VVSS) system. This obsolete suspension system was inherited from the army's early light tank designs. The vehicle was 9 feet 7 inches tall, 8 feet 9 inches wide

Chapter Three   79

In August 1941, a full-size wooden mockup of a new vehicle designated the T6 medium tank appeared, as seen in this picture taken at Aberdeen Proving Ground, Maryland. After a number of minor changes, including the removal of the hull side door, the T6 became the starting point for the entire family of "Sherman" medium tanks. During World War II, American soldiers generally referred to all the various versions of the Sherman as just the "M4." *National Archives*

Posed for a picture on June 9, 1942 is an M4A1 pilot vehicle of the Sherman. The crew of all Sherman tanks in U.S. Army service consisted of five men. The gunner was located at the right front of the turret alongside the 75-mm main gun. The vehicle commander sat or stood on a small seat just behind the gunner. The loader was on the left of the main gun where he could load it and service the .30-caliber coaxial machine gun. The driver and assistant driver sat on either side of the transmission in the front of the hull. *Michael Green*

and 20 feet 7 inches long. The maximum operating range on a full load of fuel and on level ground was about 100 miles. Crossing rougher terrain tended to use up more fuel and dramatically cut down the tank's operating range.

Gasoline engines powered all three versions of the Sherman used by the U.S. Army in combat during World War II. The M4 and M4A1 versions had large and bulky air-cooled Continental Whirlwind radial engines. Power for the M4A3 version came from a compact eight-cylinder water-cooled Ford aircraft engine. The Ford power plant was later designated the GAA engine and was the preferred engine among Sherman crews, due to its higher horsepower, better torque at low speeds, and its greater overall reliability.

The U.S. Marine Corps and Allied forces used a diesel engine version of the Sherman designated the M4A2. A small number of diesel-powered Shermans were also used by the U.S. Army for training purposes in the United States.

During World War II the Shermans proved to be a study in contrast. American wartime propaganda created the image of an invincible land battleship dashing around and blowing up or running over anything that stood in its path. A favorite slogan of the early war period stated: "We'll win the war with the M4 [Sherman]."

American tankers had a different image of the Sherman. Armor protection was weak, and the vehicle's main gun was unable to penetrate the thick armor hide on late-war German Panther and Tiger tanks. The Sherman also proved easy prey for a variety of German antitank weapons ranging from hand-held rocket launchers to powerful antitank weapons like the famous 88-mm high-velocity gun.

The Sherman was not always considered undergunned or underprotected. When it first saw combat in 1942 with the British army in North Africa, it was considered the leading edge of tank technology. High-ranking British officers stated: "The M4 [Sherman] is a better tank than the best German tank." Yet, when the invasion of Europe began in June 1944, the Sherman proved to be almost useless against superior enemy tanks.

U.S. military doctrine defined the role of the Sherman as a mass-produced exploitation vehicle designed to rush deep into the enemy's rear area to create maximum confusion and shock effect. In his letter of instruction to the Third Army dated April 3, 1944, Patton reinforced this tactical doctrine by stating:

"Battles are won by fighting the enemy. Fear is induced by inflicting death and wounds upon him. Death and wounds are produced by fire. Fire from the rear is more deadly and three times more effective than fire from the front, but to get behind the enemy, you must hold him by frontal fire and move rapidly around his flank. Frontal attacks against prepared positions should be avoided if possible."

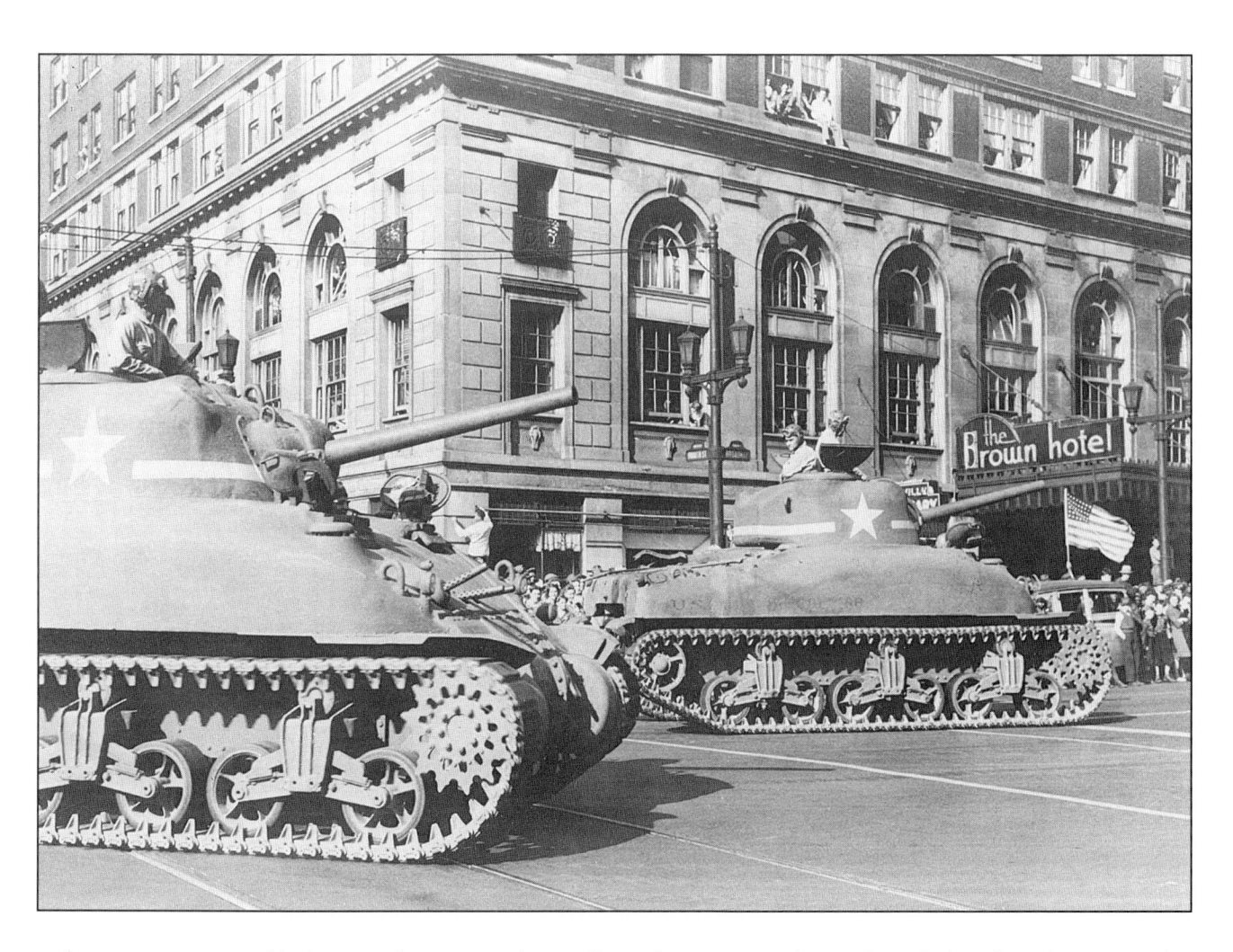

Two first-generation M4A1 versions of the Sherman are taking part in a parade in Louisville, Kentucky, on Army Day, April 6, 1942. The twin, fixed .30-caliber machine guns mounted in the lower front hull was one feature of these early production vehicles. This design feature was quickly seen as impractical for field use and was dispensed with. *National Archives*

Chapter Three 81

Pictured at the Virginia Museum of Military Vehicles is a first-generation M4A1 version of the Sherman. Clearly seen in this picture are the direct-vision slots for the driver and assistant driver positions in the front hull. All Sherman tank turrets could be traversed manually, and most could also be turned with the aid of a hydraulic system. With the hydraulic system, the turret of a Sherman could be swing through 360 degrees in 15 seconds. *Michael Green*

Coming down the production line at the Lima Locomotive Works in early 1942 are a number of first-generation versions of the M4A1 Sherman with cast steel hulls. The hulls still have the slots for the fixed twin .30-caliber machine-guns. These hulls also have the early model three-piece transmission cover, which was bolted together. Lima built 1,655 first-generation M4A1 Shermans between February 1942 and September 1943. *National Archives*

Because the army originally envisioned its Shermans being busy with rushing around an enemy's rear area positions, they were not intended to engage in combat with opposing tanks. The army wanted to leave this role to specialized tank destroyers, but combat experience soon proved this concept to be seriously flawed. The realities of battle forced the army to use its Shermans as its primary tank killers, a role they were not really designed for. Efforts to produce new tanks better suited for the job or to upgrade the Sherman to a level at which it could effectively deal with enemy tanks proved to be too little too late.

Tank Firepower

The first generation Shermans were armed with a 75-mm main gun designated M3. It was based on a towed 75-mm field gun that was first introduced into French military service in the early 1900s and was eventually adopted into U.S. Army service. Mounted in the Sherman turret, the 75-mm gun, like other tank guns then in service, fired an armor piercing (AP) round that depended on kinetic energy to punch a hole through the armor plate of an enemy tank.

The Sherman AP round was the M61. The round was capable of carrying a high-explosive (HE) element within it, but production problems caused it to be issued without the HE element until the very end of the war. AP projectiles with an HE element (M61 AP-HE rounds) were fitted with a base-detonating fuse having a delay action that would ignite the HE explosive immediately after the round penetrated the armor.

The kinetic energy (armor-piercing potential) of a projectile rises rapidly with its velocity.

Visible within the cramped confines of a first-generation Sherman turret is the seating arrangement of the vehicle commander and gunner. The gunner sits below and in front of the vehicle commander. The gunner acquires targets by looking through a periscope, which includes a telescopic sight. The effectiveness of the main gun on all tanks, from World War II until today, continues to depend on all members of the crew working together as a close-knit team. National Archives

Chapter Three   83

All first-generation Shermans used by the U.S. Army rode into battle on something called the Vertical Volute Spring Suspension (VVSS) system. It consisted of six bogie suspension assemblies, three on either side of the hull. Each bogie assembly, two of which are pictured, where made up of a horizontal spring unit mounted on an axle attached to and riding on rubber-rimmed steel bogie wheels mounted at the ends of the axle. A track return roller was mounted on the top of the bogie suspension assembly. *National Archives*

The 75-mm gun in the Sherman had a relatively poor armor-piercing performance because of its low muzzle velocity of only 2,030 feet per second. By contrast, the AP round fired by the German Panther's 75-mm main gun achieved 3,675 feet per second. The Germans also had superior ammunition and sighting telescopes, so Shermans were seldom victorious against the Panthers.

Corporal James A. Miller, a Sherman gunner, exposed his frustration in the lack of muzzle velocity in a wartime report:

"I have been in combat several times in a tank and I have found out it is silly to try to fight the German tank. One morning in Puffendorf, Germany, about daylight, I saw German tanks coming across the field toward us; we all opened fire on them, but we had just about as well have fired our shots straight up in the air for all the good we could do. Every round would bounce off and wouldn't do a bit of damage. I fired at one 800 yards away, he had his side toward me. I hit him from the lap of the turret to the bottom and from the front of the tank to the back directly in the side but he never halted. I fired one hundred and eighty four rounds at them and I hit at least five of them several times. In my opinion if we had a gun with plenty of muzzle velocity we would have wiped them out. We out-gunned them but our guns were worthless."

The 75-mm main gun of the Sherman could also fire M48 high-explosive (HE) and M89 white-phosphorous (WP) rounds. The HE and WP rounds were used against infantry and anti-tank guns. The WP round was also employed to mark targets.

The typical Sherman was also fitted with at least three machine guns. There was a coaxial .30-caliber machine gun mounted in the turret alongside the 75-mm main gun. It was used on unarmored vehicles or infantry. The Sherman gunner fired it by stepping on a foot switch. An-

Due to the very high production goals set by President Franklin D. Roosevelt for medium tanks, the Ordnance Department was forced to seek additional manufacturers for the Sherman. Since some of these companies did not have the ability to produce large hull castings, it was decided to build a welded-hull version of the Sherman, designated the M4. Pictured is a welded-hull M4 version of the Sherman at the U.S. Army's Desert Training Center in southern California. *National Archives*

other .30-caliber machine gun was mounted in the right front hull in an armored ball mount operated by the assistant driver.

A .50-caliber air-cooled M2 HB machine gun was located on the turret near the commander's cupola. This gun was capable of a maximum effective range of 1,200 yards. Muzzle velocity of the several types of ammunition fired by the M2 HB .50-caliber machine gun was 2,900 feet per second, enough to destroy lightly armored enemy vehicles.

In his general orders of May 1944, Patton stated his view on the employment of tanks in combat:

"When tanks are advancing, they must use their guns for what is known as reconnaissance by fire; that is, they must shoot at any terrestrial objective behind which an antitank gun might be concealed. They must take these targets under fire at a range greater than that at which an antitank gun is effective; in other words, at a range greater than 2,000 yards. They should fire

The Ordnance Department authorized the mounting of twin-diesel engines in the hull of a welded-hull M4 first-generation Shermans in late 1941. The modified vehicles which entered production in April 1942 was designated the M4A2. Since the U.S. Army had already decided that only gasoline-powered Shermans were to be sent overseas, most of the M4A2s were supplied to America's allies. Some M4A2 tanks saw training duties in the United States, as seen in this picture taken at Fort Knox, Kentucky. *National Archives*

Chapter Three   **85**

In late 1941 the Ordnance Department became highly interested in a liquid-cooled eight-cylinder gasoline engine for possible use in the first generation of Shermans. The power plant was a modification of an experimental Ford aircraft engine. It was designated the Ford GAA engine. Tests went very well and the engine was approved for installation in the welded-hull M4 version of the Sherman. The modified tank was designated the M4A3, with the first production vehicles rolling off the factory floor in June 1942. *National Archives*

Ford GAA tank engines were considered to be far superior to the air-cooled radial gasoline engines used in the first-generation M4 and M4A1 versions of the Sherman tank. If sufficient production capacity had existed at the time, the U.S. Army would have chosen to fit all of its Shermans with the Ford GAA engine. Some of the features that made it so popular included its high output, compactness, and excellent power-to-weight ratio. In this picture taken in the 1950s an M4A3 version of the Sherman is being used in a force-on-force training exercise. The engine exhaust grill arrangement at the rear of the vehicle is an easy spotting feature for this particular version. *National Archives*

at these targets with high-explosive or with white phosphorus. If the enemy is discovered and replies, the range will be so great as to render him ineffective.

Armor Protection

Late-war German tanks were designed for maximum firepower and armor protection at the expense of mobility. In contrast, the Sherman was designed for mobility, ease of overseas shipment, minimal logistics support, and rapid high-rate production. All these factors put firepower and protection at a much lower priority level.

The front glacis (hull) on the Sherman was 2 inches thick with the sides and rear of the hull being 1 1/2 inches thick. Most of the bottom hull plate was 1/2 inch thick, with an extra 1/2 inch at the front, where mine damage was most likely. The gun shield (mantle) on the front of the Sherman turret had a maximum thickness of 3 1/2 inches. The sides of the turret were 2-inches thick, and the roof was 1inch.

All the various versions of the Sherman had identical cast-steel armored turrets. The M4 version of the Sherman had a welded-steel armor hull and the M4A1 version a cast-steel armor

86   Armored Fighting Vehicles

hull. With its more angular shape, the welded-hull version had a bit more interior stowage space than the cast-hull version.

Tank Commander Sergeant Harold S. Rathburn described the Sherman's lack of effective armor protection in a wartime report:

"In comparing the German tank with our own medium tank, there is one thing that I would like to bring out; that is, the armor plate on each tank. The Mark V has about 4 inches on the front. The Mark VI has a little over 6 inches. When placing tank against tank, you must consider the armor of each. In past engagements with the enemy, we have placed tank against tank very often. In one tank battle, our M4 was hit in the front by an AP shell from a Mark VI. It went in the front and came out the rear. I have also seen our 75-mm AP shells bounce off the front of the Mark V and Mark VI tanks."

There were numerous reasons for the lack of heavier armor on the Sherman. Armor is the heaviest element of any tank design. Steel armor plate 1 inch thick weighs 40 pounds per square foot. When the Sherman was being developed the engineers designing the vehicle were constrained by the 35-ton load capacity of existing cranes on transport ships. In addition, portable bridges employed by the U.S. Army in the early days of the war were not designed to carry loads much greater than that of the Sherman.

To provide a little extra protection for the thin-skinned Sherman, American tank crews in Western Europe began to add to the front and sides of their vehicles almost anything that might possibly deflect an incoming enemy antitank projectile, rocket, or grenade. The materials selected for this role included everything from large wooden logs to cement-filled sandbags.

Combat experiences with the first-generation Shermans in North Africa proved to the U.S. Army that the vehicle was too thinly armored. As a short-term solution, a number of 1-inch thick steel armor plates were welded onto both the hull and turret of these tanks at the factory. These factory modifications were later dropped when newer production vehicles had been redesigned with thicker armor in key areas. The add-on armor plates can be seen both on the hull and turret of this M4A1 version of the Sherman on display at Fort Hood, Texas. *Michael Green*

Chapter Three 87

In spite of the addition of an extra armor plate on the first-generation of Shermans, the vehicle proved very easy to penetrate by enemy antitank weapons. A dramatic example of an M4A1 meeting its match is seen in this vehicle. It suffered a catastrophic explosion, which blew the turret off the hull. Such destruction normally occurred when an enemy antitank round set off the vehicle's ammunition. In such cases it was highly unlikely that the crew would survive. *Fred Ropkey collection*

Combat experience in Western Europe in 1944 and 1945 quickly proved to Sherman tankers just how poor the armor protection was on their vehicles. To compensate, tankers began adding a wide array of different materials to the outside of their vehicles to give them a little extra protection and piece of mind. The first-generation M4A3 version of the Sherman pictured features a combination of wooden logs strapped to the side of the hull and sandbags on the front hull. *National Archives*

Patton officially disapproved of the practice of adding extra armor to the Shermans used by the Third Army. He did this for a couple of different reasons. The first was the strain imposed on the automotive and suspension systems of the tanks by the added weight of the extra armor. Another reason had to do with the perception that the need for extra armor on the Sherman meant that it was not the first-rate tank that the army had professed to the American public.

The Sherman Scandal

In January 1945 Hanson Baldwin reported on the combat shortcomings of the Sherman tank in the *New York Times*:

"Why at this late stage of the war are American tanks inferior to the enemy's? That they are inferior the fighting in Normandy showed, and the recent battles in the Ardennes have again emphatically demonstrated. This has been denied, explained away and hushed up, but the men who are fighting our tanks against much heavier, better-armored and more powerfully armed German monsters know the truth. It is high time that Congress got to the bottom of a situation that does no credit to the War Department. This does not mean that our tanks are bad. They are not; they are good. They are the best tanks in the world—next to the Germans'."

In March 1945 the *Washington Post* took up the same point by asking in print why American tanks were so inferior to German tanks, the newspaper also suggesting that a serious investigation of the matter be undertaking. Patton took the official army line when questioned by American correspondents regarding the issue that same month by stating: "In mechanical endurance and ease of maintenance our tanks are infinitely superior to any other." Asked to explain what this meant in military effectiveness he pointed out that the Third Army had lost 1,136 tanks between August 1, 1944, and mid-March of 1945. In that same period it had knocked out 2,287 German tanks, of which 808 were Tigers or Panthers. "As we always have attacked," he went on, "70 percent of our casualties have been from dug-in antitank guns,

The U.S. Army had planned on fielding a new heavy tank with thicker steel armor protection than the existing Shermans by late 1944. When it became clear that this would not happen, it was decided to convert a number of first-generation M4A3 versions of the Sherman at the factory into assault tanks with extra armor on their hulls and turrets. Vehicles so modified were designated the M4A3E2. The turret on the new assault tank had sides 6 inches thick; the front hull armor was increased to 4 inches by welding on an additional 1 1/2 of armor plate. *National Archives*

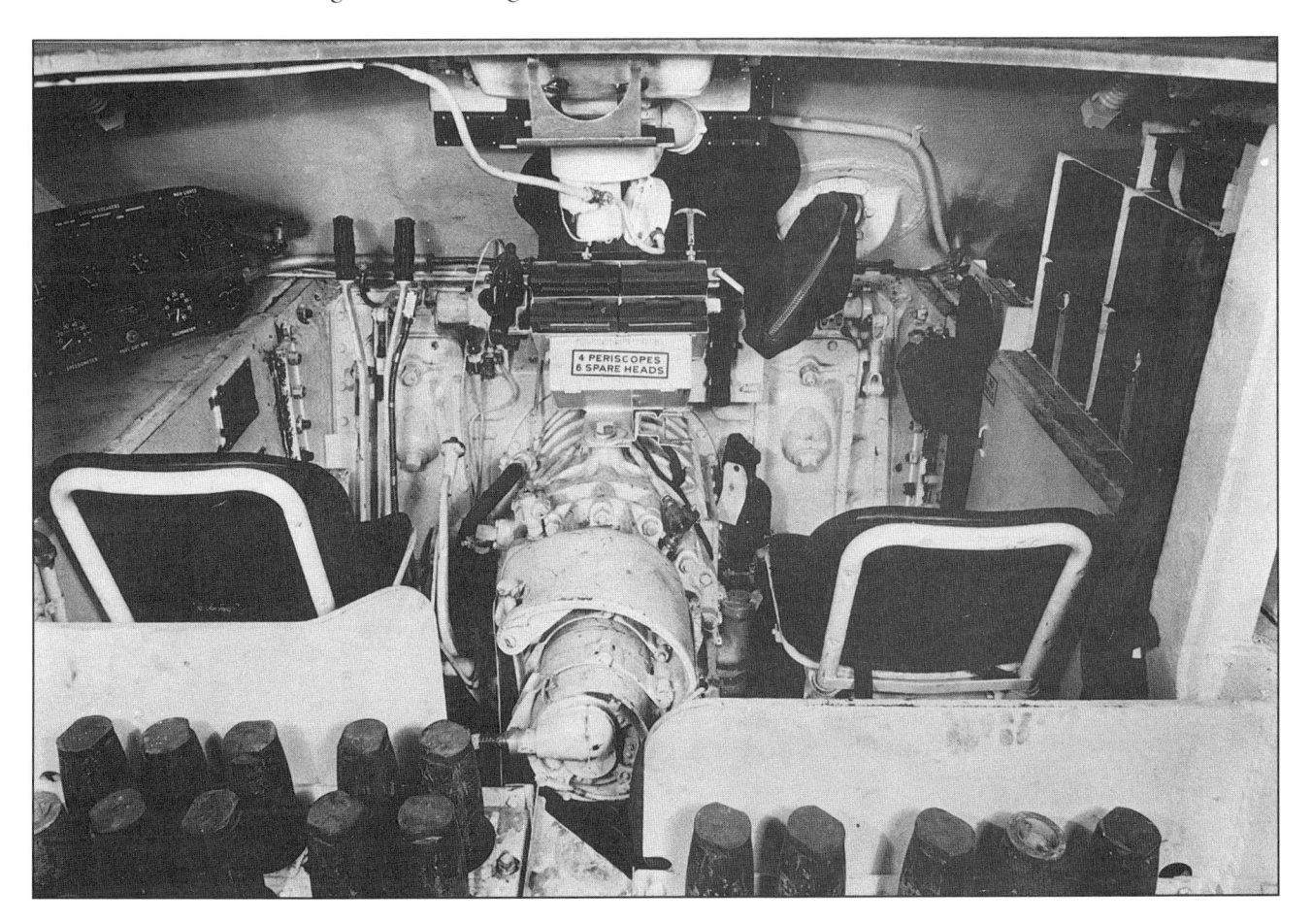

From the bottom of the turret of an M4A3E2 medium tank, this picture shows the driver's and assistant driver's seats in the front hull, with the vehicle's large transmission in the middle. The driver's two steering levers on the left side of the photograph, as well as the driver's instrument panel, can also be seen. The seating arrangement, and the placement of interior components, was identical in all the different versions of the Sherman produced during World War II. *National Archives*

Chapter Three 89

Even before the first generation of Shermans came off the assembly line, the Ordnance Department began working on modifying and improving the vehicle's design to produce a second generation. One of the main improvements was replacing the turret and 75-mm main gun on the M4A1, M4A2, and M4A3 versions of the Sherman with a new turret and a longer, more powerful 76-mm gun. Pictured is a second-generation M4A1 version of the Sherman with the new turret and gun. *National Archives*

whereas most of the enemy's tanks have been put out of action by our tanks." General Patton continued his response by remarking:

"The great mobility of the fleet-footed Sherman usually enables it to evade the slow and unwieldy Tiger. With their adoption of this cumbersome tank, the German, in my judgment, lost much of his ability in armored combat. These tanks are so heavy and their road life so short that the German is driven to use them as guns rather than as tanks. That is, he is forced on the defensive against our armor, whereas we invariably try and generally succeed in using our armor on the offensive against his infantry, communications and supply lines, the proper use of armor.

Had the armored division that accompanied the Third Army across France been equipped with Tigers, the road losses would have been 100 percent by the time we reached the Moselle River. As it was, our road losses were negligible.

In current operations, had the Fourth Armored Division been equipped with Tiger or Panther tanks and been required to make the move from Saarguemines to Arlon, thence through Bastogne, from Bastogne to the Rhine and now to Mainz, it would have been necessary to rearmor it twice, and we should have had serious trouble in crossing the rivers."

The second-generation M4A3 version of the Sherman armed with the new turret and 76-mm main gun first appeared in service in March 1944. By the end of August 1944, a total of 1,400 had been produced. These vehicles had all the second-generation improvements but still rode into battle on the older style VVSS system. *National Archives*

90   **Armored Fighting Vehicles**

Despite Patton's public remarks regarding the superiority of the Sherman in comparison to late war German tanks, both he and the army knew that something had be done to improve the odds between American and German tankers. One early attempt to improve the armor protection on the Sherman began in February 1944, when the Ordnance Department began considering the possibility of adding extra armor protection in the field to both light and medium tanks for the infantry support (assault) role. While this idea was eventually dismissed as unworkable, Ordnance began looking at adding armor to the Sherman during production.

Starting with production models of the M4A3 version of the Sherman in May of 1944, the hull and turret armor on a number of vehicles was increased to that required for the assault tank role. The extra armor weight required upgrading of the vehicle's suspension and powertrain. A total of 254 such assault tanks, redesignated M4A3E2, were produced in just three months.

The first shipment arrived in Western Europe in late 1944 and served successfully for the remainder of the war. The popular nickname for the M4A3E2 among American tankers in Europe was the "Jumbo."

Patton stated his opinion on the need for additional armor on the Sherman in a 1944 report:

"While this is probably not the proper place to bring it out, it is my opinion that the most important development for armor is not a bigger gun or thicker armor, but better armor which weighs less. It may well be that a judicious combination of armor and plastic will be the answer to this problem."

Upgrading the Sherman

Before the first generation of Shermans even came off the assembly line in February of 1942, the Ordnance Department had already begun work on a major redesign of the vehicle. Improvements would include a new suspension system, thicker

A second-generation M4A3 version of the Sherman has fallen into a large bomb crater. Clearly visible is the very long barrel of the vehicle's 76-mm main gun. Also visible are the various crew hatches. The vehicle commander's hatch contained six periscopes that were bulletproof against heavy machine gun fire. *National Archives*

Chapter Three 91

armor, new ammunition storage arrangements, upgraded driver's hatches, and turret vision blocks for the tank commander. The first of these new and improved second-generation Shermans appeared in early 1944. The various improvements added an extra two tons of weight to the vehicles.

The most distinguishing outward characteristic of the upgraded second generation of Shermans was the new horizontal volute spring suspension (HVSS) system with its wider, heavier double-pin steel track. The suspension system improved cross-country mobility even though the vehicle weight was greater.

At the same time the second-generation Sherman was coming to fruition, a new 76-mm main gun was being phased into service. The gun embodied the same physical characteristics as the M3 75-mm guns originally mounted in the first generation of Shermans but had a longer gun tube, giving it a higher muzzle velocity and, therefore, greater striking power and a

Another important design feature seen on all later versions of the second generation of Shermans was the incorporation of an improved suspension system, designated the horizontal volute spring suspension (HVSS) system. The second-generation M4A3 version of the Sherman pictured has the HVSS system fitted. *National Archives*

Second-generation M4A3 versions of the Sherman with the 76-mm main gun armed turret, and riding on the HVSS system, were the final production version of the vehicle in U.S. Army service. Early pilot vehicles were designated the M4A3E8 during the Ordnance Department testing process. Troops involved in the tests nicknamed it the "Easy Eight," which later stuck to the vehicle in field use. Production examples were designated the M4A3(76)W HVSS. The capital letter "W" designated a vehicle with an antifreeze-filled ammunition storage system. *National Archives*

92   Armored Fighting Vehicles

The suspension system as seen on this second-generation M4A3(76)W HVSS Sherman featured 23-inch wide-tracks with the use of center guides. The first generation of Shermans with the VVSS system had narrower 16 9/16-inch tracks and outside guides. The much wider tracks on second-generation Shermans greatly improved their riding qualities as well as durability. The wide track did require the use of dual bogie wheels on the second-generation vehicles. *National Archives*

Chapter Three

longer effective range. Testing of the new gun began in August of 1942. Early test results were so encouraging that the gun was approved for production only one month after tests had started. The new gun was designated M1, and was followed almost immediately by an improved version designated M1A1. With the addition of a muzzle brake, the M1A1 was redesignated M1A1C. Another version with different rifling was known as the M1A2.

The Ordnance Department installed an M1A1 76-mm gun in the preproduction turret and gun mount of an experimental medium tank turret known as the T23. It was soon decided to make more productive use of the new gun and turret and mount them on a first generation M4 version of the Sherman. This vehicle configuration was designated M4E6. The M4E6 fired an M62 APC (armored piercing capped) round. Later versions of this round contained an HE filler and a base-detonating delay fuse designed to explode within the target. The M62 APC round fired from the 76-mm main gun achieved a muzzle velocity of 2,600 feet per second compared to the 2,030 feet per second of the 75-mm gun found in the first-generation of Shermans.

The army's original plans had called for mounting its new up-gunned turrets on the M4, M4A1 and M4A3 versions of its second-generation Shermans. However, with invasion plans for the continent well under way, the army started installing the new up-gunned turrets on late-production, first-generation Shermans that were still coming off the assembly lines.

The Pressed Steel Car Company finished production of the first 100 M4A1 models of the first-generation Sherman with the up-gunned turret in January 1944. These vehicles were designated M4A1(76)W. The letter designation W was short

Because of the greater width of the HVSS system, a running board was placed on each side of the hull. Many vehicles with the running board were also equipped with sand shields, as visible in this picture of an M4A3(76)W HVSS Sherman. Sand shields were used to keep down the amount of dust and dirt from being thrown up by the vehicle when moving. *National Archives*

94   Armored Fighting Vehicles

An interesting comparison photo shows the many visible differences between the two generations of Sherman tanks. On the right is a first-generation welded-hull M4A3 version of the Sherman, armed with a 75-mm main gun and riding on the narrow VVSS system. On the left is a second-generation cast-hull M4A1 version, an armed with a 76-mm main gun and fitted with the much wider HVSS system. Both vehicles belong to the Indiana Museum of Military History, founded by Fred Ropkey. *Michael Green*

for Wet, referring to Sherman tanks fitted with newly designed main gun storage bins containing antifreeze. The antifreeze was intended to stop or inhibit ammunition fires when an enemy AP round penetrated a tank.

The Pressed Steel Car Company eventually began production of a second-generation M4A1 model of the Sherman with the up-gunned turret and the new HVSS suspension system. These vehicles were designated M4A1(76)W HVSS. The Pressed Steel Car Company built more than 3,400 units before the war ended.

Chrysler started production of the first generation of M4A3 models armed with the up-gunned turret in March of 1944. By August 1944, Chrysler had completely phased in the second-generation models of the M4A3 armed with the up-gunned turret. These vehicles were designated M4A3(76)W HVSS. American tankers normally referred to the vehicle by its earlier designations as the M4A3E8 or by its popular nickname the "Easy Eight." First Lieutenant Ural E. Oyler, a platoon leader, commented in a World War II report about his impressions of the new Easy Eight tank entering service in early 1945:

"The new M4A3E8 has so far proved very successful in operation. It has the desirable features except a bit of added armor plate on the front and on the forward side of the turret."

Patton quietly gave permission in early 1945 for a number of M4A3E8 tanks in the Third Army to be upgraded with extra armor plate similar to that found on the M4A3E2 "Jumbo" assault tanks. To provide the extra armor plate needed to up-armor the existing M4A3E8 tanks, the Third Army workshops were given permission to cut up damaged late-war second-generation Shermans with welded hulls, and place their armor plate on undamaged tanks. The fact that this was even occurring was kept quiet, since the cannibalized Shermans could never be rebuilt.

Chapter Three 95

Combat Effectiveness

A small number of first-generation M4A1 model tanks armed with the up-gunned turrets were delivered to England before the invasion of France. Firing demonstrations were arranged for senior American officers. Everyone who saw the demonstrations came away impressed. Yet, most of the officers decided that they would rather stick with the familiar 75-mm gun already mounted in their Shermans than to retrain their troops on a new gun. Even Patton refused to take the new gun into battle unless it was successfully tested in combat.

This lack of interest in a bigger and supposedly better gun for the Sherman seems strange in hindsight. However, at the time, most army commanders retained their faith in the effectiveness of the 75-mm gun. Combat in North Africa and fighting in Sicily and Italy had shown that the first generation of Shermans compared well with the German tanks then in service. While a small number of German Tiger I tanks saw action in both North Africa and later in Sicily and Italy, poor tactics and difficult terrain limited their effectiveness, giving American tankers a false sense of security. The German Panther tank saw limited action in Italy, but it also failed to generate any doubts in the ability of the first generation of Shermans armed with the 75-mm gun to succeed in battle.

The first hint of real trouble for Shermans armed with the 75-mm gun began in the southern Normandy countryside in June 1944, when they first encountered German Panther tanks. American tank crews soon discovered that their 75-mm gun was almost completely useless against the Panther's thick and well-sloped frontal armor. Even the few 76-mm gun Shermans in service proved to be unable to penetrate the Panther's thick armor. When this news reached General Dwight Eisenhower he commented in frustration:

"You mean our 76 won't knock these Panthers out? I thought it was going to be the wonder gun of the war. Why is it that I am always the last to hear about this stuff? Ordnance told me this 76 would take care of anything the Germans had. Now I find you can't knock out a damn thing with it."

The 76-mm gun's inability to penetrate the frontal armor of German tanks can be blamed squarely on the Ordnance Department. It was Ordnance's failure to correctly assess the protection level of German mechanized armor that led to the deployment of weapons like the 76-mm gun.

In September 1943, Armored Force commander Major General Alvan C. Gillem wrote a

An American tanker poses next to his M4A3(76)W Sherman with its frontal hull plate covered with a combination of cement-filled sandbags overlain and held in place by a layer of poured concrete. The wooden planks at the bottom of the front hull were used to hold the concrete as it dried. To retain the use of the front hull-mounted .30-caliber machine gun, the crew made a small opening with a metal pipe through the concrete. *National Archives*

letter to the Army Ground Forces commander, General Lesley J. McNair. In that letter he stated that figures supplied by the Ordnance Department confirmed that the 76-mm gun should have been able to penetrate the frontal armor of the Tiger tank at a range of 2,000 yards. In truth, the 76-mm gun was only able to penetrate a Tiger tank's frontal armor at a tactically useless 50 yards or less.

In a wartime report, Sergeant Nick Moceri summed up the feelings shared by the majority of American tankers in Western Europe in 1944 and 1945:

"I've been told that the M4A3 tank [with the 76-mm gun] is the equal if not a better tank than the German Mark V Panther. That's not so! The only reason that we've gone as far as we have is summed up in 'Quantity and the Cooperation of Arms.' Until such time as the army puts out a tank gun that can knock out a Panther from the front at 1,500 yards, or adds enough armor to stop a shell from the same distance, we'll continue to lose a heavy toll of tanks, men and equipment."

To increase the lethality of the 76-mm gun, the Ordnance Department gave high priority to the development of better ammunition for the weapon. The end result was a new 76-mm high-velocity armor piercing (HVAP) round using a tungsten-carbide tip encased in aluminum to prevent the hard but brittle tip from shattering on impact. Limited supplies of these HVAP rounds were rushed to the tankers in the field. The intention was to supply each 76-mm gun on an Sherman with a small number of these special rounds.

Major Paul A. Bane Jr. discussed the reality of the situation in a wartime report:

"Our tank crews have had some success with the HVAP 76-mm ammunition. However, at no time have we been able to secure more than five rounds per tank, and in recent actions this has been reduced to a maximum of two rounds. In many tanks all this type has been expended without being replaced."

The scarce HVAP round was better, but it was still not enough to defeat Tiger tanks at realistic ranges. First Lieutenant William L.

This M4A3(76)W HVSS Sherman pictured in Europe in early 1945 features an add-on armor kit welded onto its front hull. The add-on armor extends all the way down to the cast front-mounted transmission housing. Besides the standard .50-caliber machine gun seen behind the vehicle commander, the crew of this vehicle has placed a .30-caliber machine gun in front of the loader's hatch. *National Archives*

Chapter Three 97

U.S. Army Observations on the German Mark V Panther Tank

The following characteristics of the Panther compared to the M4A3E8 HVSS Sherman were based on the results of tests conducted by the Second Armored Division in 1945 with captured Panther tanks (Model Ausf. G).

Speed —The Mark V had a maximum speed of 18 miles per hour over terrain where tracks sank approximately 1 inch. The M4A3E8's speed was approximately the same. Some individual M4A3E8s were found that could outrun the Mark V in a speed test, while others fell slightly behind. The maximum speed of the Mark V on hard-surfaced highway was 38 miles per hour. No comparison was made with the M4A3E8 on the road.

Turret Speed —When power driven, the turret traversing speed was one-half that of the M4A3E8. Manual traversing speed depended on the operator, but the Mark V was in all cases slower than any American tank, and very difficult except when the tank was level.

Trafficability— Operating across typical ground, the Mark V left a track imprint 1/2-inch deep. It did not break through the ground surface. Similar results were obtained with the M4A3E8. Other tanks of the M4 series with narrow track and no track extension broke through the ground surface, leaving a tank imprint 2 inches deep.

Maneuverability— From a standstill, the Mark V can turn around without forward movement by locking one track. All drivers agreed that in movement, especially on roads and in built-up areas, American tanks were somewhat easier to handle and more maneuverable.

Gasoline Consumption —Tank capacity of the Mark V Tank is 135 gallons; consumption cross-country: approximately 3 gallons per mile; consumption on highway: approximately 2 gallons per mile. American gasoline was satisfactory without any readjustments of time or carburetor.

Maintenance

1. Tracks. Track blocks are removed by knocking out two drift pins. Track tension is adjusted by turning one large nut. Crews agreed that track adjustment and maintenance were easier on the Mark V than American tanks. During approximately 75 miles of operation, both on roads and cross-country, tracks have given no trouble except for track guides. These were broken when the tank was recovered.
2. Lubrication. A master grease fitting inside the turret lubricates all bearings in the tank. This is a desirable feature.
3. Radiators. There are four radiators under the rear deck with total capacity of 35 gallons. These are vulnerable to shell fragments and strafing through openings on back deck.
4. Engine. The power plant has required no maintenance other than first echelon. The repair or replacement of any part would require complete removal of the engine from the housing. Continual operation at high speed across difficult terrain causes overheating within one-half hour.

Stowage

1. Ammunition. Place is provided for 73 rounds of 75-mm ammunition. Ammunition is accessible. The capacity for the two machine guns could not be determined.
2. Equipment. Personal equipment, blankets, field bags, etc., was found stowed in a box on the outside. The turret has more space inside than the American M4 series. The space in the driver's and assistant driver's compartment is approximately the same in the two tanks. Drivers' seats not readily adjustable as in our tanks.

Visibility—When buttoned up, the assistant driver and loader see through periscopes fixed to the right oblique. The driver has a flexible periscope. The gunner has vision only through the telescope sight. The tank commander has all-around vision. The M4A3E8 has greater visibility than the Mark V, which is comparatively blind when buttoned up.

Fordability —The Mark V tank forded water to a depth of 59 inches. Although it would take greater depth for a short time (up to 70 inches), there was a tendency for water to splash through the fan openings in the top deck. The M4A3E8 forded water safely up to 30 inches. It could ford up to 36 inches, but water tended to splash into the exhaust.

Gun and Sights —The telescopic sight on the 75-mm gun of the Mark V tank is adjustable. By pushing a lever on the sight's right side, the magnifying power is controlled, there being two settings, two and six power. There is also an adjustable reticle in the sight (used in setting off the range) and a simple, effective antiglare device.

—The 75-mm gun is fired electrically and cannot be fired manually. There are tubes fitted inside the breech which blow the powder gasses out the tube before the breech is opened, and thus prevent fouling the air inside the fighting compartment.

Comparative Weight of Projectiles—
76-mm APC 15.59 pounds
    90-mm APC 24.55 pounds
    75-mm (Mark V) 15.70 pounds

—It is interesting to note that while the weight of our 76-mm projectile and that of the German 75-mm are almost identical, the shell case of the 75-mm slightly longer and greater in diameter than our 90-mm shell case. It delivers an almost flat trajectory for extremely effective AT range and incredible accuracy.

Strengths
1. Heavy armor on front slope plate.
2. High-velocity weapon (75-mm) with excellent sights.
3. Good cross-country mobility, but no better than the M4A3E8.
4. Easy track adjustment and track maintenance.
5. High fordability and ease of preparation for amphibious operations.

Weaknesses
1. Because of no periscope sight for the gunner and lack of the gyrostabilizer on the Mark V, firing with any accuracy during movement would be impossible.
2. Limited visibility of crew members.
3. Slow traversing speed of turret.
4. Overheating of engine during difficult operation.
5. Bright glow of exhaust stacks at night after engine runs for a short period.
6. Difficulty in performing maintenance on engine.
7. Thin armor plate (5/8 inch) over driver and engine compartment.
8. Large openings on top of rear deck for cooling fans vulnerable to shellfire and strafing.
9. Lack of gyrostabilizer.
10. Lack of escape hatch.
11. Heavy gasoline consumption.
12. No control of turret traverse by tank commander, only by the gunner.
13. No AA (antiaircraft) gun provided.

Schaubel described the performance of HVAP in a wartime report:

"At Oberemot, Germany, 27 February 1945, our second platoon on roadblock was engaged by two Tiger tanks, Mark VI, at 3,600 yards, and two of our Shermans were knocked out. Our 3,400-feet-per-second 76-mm HVAP ammunition was used and bounced off the side slopes, seven rounds. Definitely out-ranged due to better sights in the Mark VI and more muzzle velocity in their souped-up ammunition. Upon throwing smoke at the Tiger tanks, they withdrew because smoke means marking target for artillery and fighter-bombers to the Germans."

Confronted by the fact that even the special HVAP fired from 76-mm gun-equipped Shermans was not up to the job of destroying German tanks, the morale of American tankers sank even lower. One tanker remarked: "The Germans have been improving steadily ever since we met them in Sicily. Our [Ordnance] Department needs to get on the ball!"

The only positive note for American tankers in late 1944 and early 1945 was the impressive kill ratio attained by M36 tank destroyers armed with the M3 90-mm gun—a modified antiaircraft gun. Embarrassing questions about the reasons for not mounting these 90-mm guns on Shermans were soon being asked in Europe and in the United States.

The troops did not know that the Ordnance Department had demonstrated a Sherman

The U.S. Army-supplied add-on armor kits that appeared late in World War II were originally designed to be fitted only on welded-hull M4 versions of the Sherman that had the redesigned 47-degree welded-hull front. American tankers who were equipped with the cast-hull M4A1 version of the Sherman decided they also needed the extra protection offered by these add-on armor kits. The crew of the M4A1(76)W Sherman pictured has attached two of the add-on armor plates together and mounted them on the front hull of their vehicle. *National Archives*

armed with a 90-mm gun to one of Eisenhower's senior staff shortly after the invasion of Europe. This was at a time when it was already clear to all personnel stationed in France that a heavily armed American tank was essential. Even so, when Eisenhower's staff member expressed interest in the test vehicle, the Ordnance Department discouraged him. They informed him that the Sherman could not support the heavier gun system. According to the Ordnance Department the troops in France would be better served by waiting for the arrival of the new T26 heavy tank armed with a 90-mm main gun due in late 1944. Based on this planned delivery date, the Ordnance Department believed there was no pressing need to upgrade the Sherman to support the 90-mm gun.

The Army Ground Forces also showed interest in a 90-mm gun carried by a Sherman, but senior army officers were still convinced that the destruction of enemy tanks was better accomplished by specialized tank destroyers like the M36. By the time that this belief had been repeatedly proven wrong, it was too late to put such a vehicle into production.

In a classic case of too little too late, Patton's Third Army received its first shipment of 30 M26 Pershing heavy tanks in April of 1945—a few weeks before Germany surrendered. The 45-ton Pershing was everything that the M4 series tanks were not. It was heavily armored and carried a powerful M3 90-mm gun that could destroy both Panther and Tiger tanks from relatively normal battle ranges.

Each of the 30 M26 Pershing heavy tanks that first appeared in the service of Patton's Third Army in late April 1945 had a crew of five men and weighed 45 tons. They were 22 feet 4 inches long (excluding gun), 11 feet 6 inches wide, and 9 feet 1 inch tall. Of the 310 M26 Pershing tanks that made it to Europe before Germany surrendered in the first week of May 1945, only 20 saw combat action. *National Archives*

Chapter Three 101

American tankers in Western Europe had eagerly awaited the promised M26 heavy tank throughout late 1944 and early 1945. An example of their interest in a vehicle that could effectively deal with German tanks is seen in the comments of a tank sergeant who stated in a World War II report:

"I have never seen the M26 with the 90-mm gun on it, but if it is as good as the one on the T.D. [tank destroyers] it is the answer to a tankman's prayer. Against the Mark V our T.D. with a 90-mm gun are pretty good but our guns don't stand up to the Jerry guns.

"My opinion on the sights, tracks, engine, gun, and maneuverability is that our sights could be improved a lot, and if that M26 has wide tracks and a more powerful engine it would give us speed and maneuverability and with our added firepower we would have some chance of living. As we go now every man has resigned himself to dying sooner or later because we don't have a chance against the German tanks. All of this stuff that we read about German tanks knocked out by our tanks makes us sick because we know what prices we have to pay in men and equipment to accomplish it."

The sad state of American tank development before and during World War II was caused by fundamental mistakes on strategy made at the top levels of the army. Poor technical intelligence gathering and senior officers who allowed their personal agendas to interfere with what they knew the troops in the field really needed only made matters worse.

Of the many agencies involved in tank design and development, the Ordnance Department showed the greatest lack of vision. Patton neatly summed up the feeling of many American tankers when he told an Ordnance officer that "Ordnance takes too God damn long seeking perfection at the expense of the fighting men, and you can tell that to anybody at Ordnance."

The well-sloped armor arrangement of the German Panther medium tank is clearly evident in this picture of an early production model captured in Italy in 1944. *National Archives*

102   Armored Fighting Vehicles

Chapter Four

ANTITANK WEAPONS

When the British army introduced the first tanks into combat during World War I, they were firmly convinced that there was no need for special antitank weapons. Artillery would be enough to successfully deal with any enemy tanks on the battlefield. The pamphlet (reprinted in 1918 by the U.S. War Department) pointed out that the tank's only purpose was to support infantry during both offensive and defensive maneuvers. This theory became ingrained U.S. Army doctrine for the next 20 years.

The appearance of the German army's first armored (panzer) divisions in 1935 forced the American army to rethink this position. The German army regarded the tank

Ready for an offensive operation somewhere in France during the summer of 1940 is part of a German armored (panzer) division. In the foreground are a number of light and medium tanks. In the background are numerous wheeled support vehicles. Impressive scenes such as this made the U.S. Army seriously think about improving its antitank defensive measures. *British Army Tank Museum*

Chapter Four   103

Up until the early 1930s, the U.S. Army's principal antitank weapon was a small variation of the towed 37-mm gun designed by the French in 1885. It is pictured here being pulled into action by its crew sometime in the late 1920s. The Americans bought 620 such French-built for use by their troops in France in 1917. Over 3,000 American-built copies, designated the M1916, were built in 1918. Only a handful of the American-built copies saw service before the war in Europe ended. *National Archives*

as an important offensive weapon to be employed in massed formations on the front lines of every battle. Instead of traveling at the walking pace of an infantryman, German tanks took advantage of their speed to dash deep behind enemy lines and disrupt rear area headquarters, communications, and supply units. As a result of these tactics, strategists in the U.S. Army soon began planning for specialized antitank units within its infantry divisions.

However, the U.S. Army lacked a suitable antitank gun for the infantry. During the period between the two world wars, research and development funding for antitank guns was virtually nonexistent. The only U.S. Army infantry weapon that was even considered as having a limited antitank role in the period right after World War I was a small French-designed and -built 37-mm cannon generally referred to as the "Trench Gun." The U.S. Army had acquired roughly 3,000 examples of the Trench Gun in 1918. By 1929 the army had an American-built version in service with the designation 37-mm Gun M2. Due to its short range and the small shell, it was pulled from service in the early 1930s, leaving the army without any antitank guns. The army was forced to look at foreign sources for a proven weapon design that could be introduced into service quickly.

In December 1935, positive reports from an American military observer in Berlin regarding a German-made 37-mm antitank gun resulted in the U.S. Ordnance Department buying an example. The small towed weapon was known in German army service as the Pak (antitank) 36. In 1937, the Pak 36 was tested against an experimental American 37-mm gun, a French 25-mm gun and a German 47-mm gun.

The U.S. Army took the results of the shoot-out and adopted a highly modified version of the German 37-mm antitank gun. The gun was adapted to a towed platform and, with the barrel shortened by 6 inches, became the main armament on the new light and medium tanks. The

Pictured in a 1920s U.S. Army training exercise is a French-designed 37-mm Gun M1916 alongside a British designed Stokes Mortar. The 37-mm gun could fire a 1.25-1/4-pound armor piercing (AP) shot projectile that could penetrate 0.7 inches of armor plate at 2,500 yards. Maximum range of the gun was two miles, and at 1,000 yards it was more accurate than a rifle. Armor piercing projectiles having no high-explosive filler are called "shot." *National Archives*

German soldiers are pictured rushing their 37-mm Pak 36 antitank gun into action. The Pak 36 weighed 952 pounds and fired a 1.5-pound AP projectile at a muzzle velocity of 2,500 feet per second to a maximum range of 4,400 yards. The actual range at which any antitank gun could successfully penetrate enemy armor (called its effective range) was a great deal less than its maximum range. *British Army Tank Museum*

Chapter Four   105

tank gun was designated M5, and it later became M6 after a change in the breech mechanism.

The towed version was designated M3 and was soon changed to M3A1 when the muzzle brake was removed in late 1939.

The M3A1 on its two-wheel carriage weighed 912 pounds—well within the 1,000-pound weight limit that allowed antitank guns to be moved by their crews without powered equipment. This shortsighted and firm requirement effectively precluded the infantry branch from considering a more effective large-caliber antitank gun.

More remarkable is that during the four years it took to place the M3A1 into service, the infantry branch was informed that the gun had become incapable of defeating new developments in enemy armor. Yet, the decision to push the gun into production was not rescinded. Making matters even worse, in August 1938 the War Department cut off funding for the development of a larger antitank gun. The chief of the artillery branch of the Manufacturing Division from 1937 to 1939 later stated:

"The Ordnance Department was well aware that the 37-mm gun was totally inadequate as an antitank gun, and many and repeated efforts were made to convince the various interested using service personnel of the fact. It is my opinion that all of the early artillery of World War II . . . suffered from the continued insistence by the using arms on mobility, even at the expense of striking power."

The U.S. Army's Ordnance Department also made some shortsighted decisions before World War II regarding antitank gun development. In December 1938, the chief of field artillery, citing reports from overseas observers about antitank gun development in Europe, requested that the War Department fund the development of a truck-mounted antitank gun of undetermined caliber to be used by the field artillery.

The chief of ordnance objected to the plan, stating that the introduction of yet another gun into service with new types of ammunition would complicate production and supply. He also believed that existing 75-mm howitzers and 75-mm field guns could effectively supplement the yet-to-be-fielded M3 37-mm antitank gun in stopping tanks. Based on the objections of the ordnance chief, the field artillery withdrew its request, thus killing any last-minute chance that the army could deploy an effective antitank gun early in World War II.

The American-built 37-mm Gun M3A1 on its two-wheel, split-trail carriage weighed 990 pounds. It fired either a 1.92-pound AP shot or an armor piercing capped (APC) shot with a muzzle velocity of 2,900 feet. The term "capped" refers to a blunt steel nose cap with a hard face and a relatively soft core that was placed over the point of steel shot projectile. Crew protection came from a thin armored gun shield. National Archives

Pictured during a training exercise in the early 1940s are crew members of a U.S. Army 37-mm Gun M3A1, who have camouflaged their antitank weapon with some local vegetation. The main role of the blunt steel nose cap in an APC shot or projectile was to prevent the tip of the shot or projectile from shattering on impact, or bouncing off (ricocheting) an armor-plated target. *National Archives*

The 75-mm Pack Howitzer M1A1, described by the chief of ordnance as having an antitank capability, had been in army service since 1927. It was a well-liked weapon that would see much use during World War II. However, its low muzzle velocity (1,250 feet per second) made it ineffective on the battlefield of the 1940s as an antitank weapon.

The M1897A2 75-mm field gun was a French weapon left over from World War I. It first entered French military service in 1898 and was the world's first quick-firing field gun. In World War I, the "French 75" was the standard field gun of both the French army and the American Expeditionary Force (AEF) in France.

The M1897A2 remained as the mainstay of the U.S. Army field artillery until early World War II. Half-hearted modernization efforts included replacement of the wooden spoke wheels with roller bearings and pneumatic tires, and improvement of the primitive carriage with split trails that increased the gun's range, angle of elevation, and traverse. Guns so modified were designated as the M1897A4.

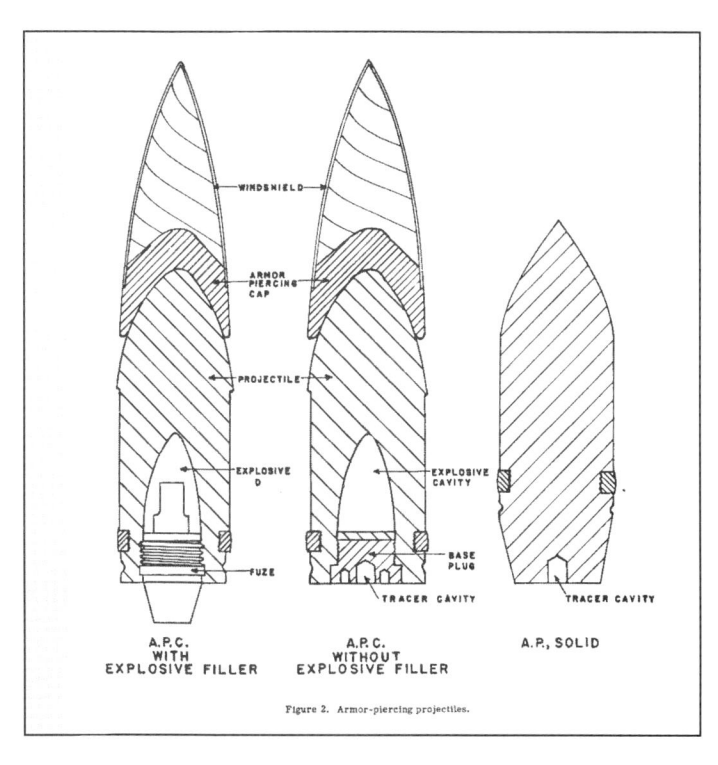

Early in World War II the U.S. Army decided to depend on APC shot rather than AP shot in its tanks and antitank weapons. APC shot was generally more effective against face-hardened armor plates than sloped homogeneous armor plate. With the midwar introduction of German tanks with sloped homogeneous armor, the effectiveness of American APC shots dropped. It was only in the last year of the war that an APC projectile with a high-explosive filler and base-denoting fuse appeared in U.S. Army service. It was designated as APC-HE. Shown in this line drawing are cutaway side views of the different types of shells used in U.S. Army tanks in World War II.

Chapter Four   **107**

Pictured is a 75-mm Gun M1897 being towed by a 4x4 U.S. Army truck in the late 1930s. When an APC shot or projectile struck an armored target, the blunt steel nose cap absorbed most of the impact force by transmitting it along the shoulders of the steel shot or projectile. This action relieved the tip of the shot or projectile from stress and helped to maintain its structural integrity. *National Archives*

The U.S. Army crew of a 75-mm Gun M1897 (also called the French 75) is loading its weapon for a firing mission during a training exercise in the United States during the late 1930s. In the process of striking an armored target, the softer core of an APC shot or projectile deformed (flattened) over the armor plate of its target. It therefore acted as a support and a lubricant as the main steel body of the shot or projectile attempted to penetrate the armor. *National Archives*

108   Antitank Weapons

Reality Sets In

In September 1939, six panzer divisions led the German army across the Polish border and in a month's time destroyed Poland's military, forcing the country to surrender. This spectacular success alarmed senior military staffs of France, Great Britain, and the United States. However, they tempered their concerns somewhat, by dismissing the Polish army as a second-rate opponent and not a true test of the effectiveness of the German panzer divisions. However, the German attack on Poland was the catalyst that caused Congress to fund a long-delayed rearmament program.

In May 1940 the Germans did it again. This time, 10 panzer divisions led the successful German invasion of France. In a span of only a few days, the French army, considered the finest in the world, disintegrated in the face of the German onslaught. France agreed to an armistice a few weeks later. Even though each French infantry division was armed with 58 fixed-position antitank guns, it became abundantly clear that the overall Allied antitank strategy was seriously flawed. American infantry divisions were hopelessly equipped with a mere 24 antitank guns. As if it were necessary, large-scale U.S. Army maneuvers in the fall of 1940 reinforced the fact that fixed-position antitank guns in defensive positions were useless against massed tank attacks. Immediately following these maneuvers, the War Department directed that only a few antitank guns should be placed in fixed positions. The bulk of the antitank guns should be held as mobile reserves. This shift in doctrine had been suggested months earlier by the French after their defeat in July 1940.

Despite French military warnings and U.S. War Department directives, the army showed little interest in changing its antitank doctrine. On April 12, 1941, Major General Lesley J. McNair, commander of the Army Ground Forces, showed his frustration with the entire issue when he wrote:

"It is beyond belief that so little could be done on the question in view of all that has happened abroad. I for one have missed no opportunity to hammer for something real in the way of antitank defense, but so far have gotten nowhere. I have no reason now to feel encouraged, but can only hope this apathy will not continue indefinitely."

Partly in reaction to McNair's comments, the army's Chief of Staff General George C. Marshall issued a memo on April 14, 1941, directing that "prompt consideration be given to the creation of

In their winter uniforms, the American crew of a "French 75" prepare for a firing mission. Because of the poor aerodynamic shape of the steel-nose caps found in American-made APC shots, they had a very poor ballistic performance in flight. To rectify this problem a thin steel windshield, also known as a ballistic cap, was generally secured to the cap or the head of the shot or projectile to improve flight performance. *National Archives*

A crew of a British Army Six-Pounder Mark II antitank gun is pictured in North Africa in 1942 awaiting an attack by German tanks. Developed in 1938, this antitank gun did not enter service until late 1941. The weapon was originally provided with a roughly six-pound AP shot, which left the barrel with a muzzle velocity of 2,675 feet per second. As the armor on German tanks improved, more advanced AP ammunition was developed for the gun, allowing it to remain a potent weapon till the end of the war. *British Army Tank Museum*

highly mobile antitank-antiaircraft units as corps and army troops for use in meeting mechanized units. These units to be in addition to organic [divisional] antitank weapons."

The 57-mm Antitank Gun

The Ordnance Department was not completely averse to improving antitank weapons during this period. Following the French debacle, the Ordnance Department found a replacement for its 20,000 M3A1 37-mm antitank guns in the British 57-mm antitank gun known as the six-pounder. (In British military terminology artillery pieces and antitank guns are not described by the bore diameter, but rather by the weight of the shell fired). The six-pounder had so far proven very effective against German tanks during the fighting in North Africa.

Due to a lack of production facilities in England to build the six-pounder, the British government authorized gun production in the United States in February 1941. The Ordnance Department started building an American version of the six-pounder, designated 57-mm Gun

Crewmen of a U.S. Army 57-mm Antitank Gun M1 have taken up position in the center of a badly damaged French city in September 1944. This American-built copy of the British-designed six-pounder antitank gun fired a 7.23-pound APC projectile at a muzzle velocity of 2,800 feet per second. The barrel on the American weapon was 16 inches longer than that of the British version of the gun, giving it a slightly higher muzzle velocity. *National Archives*

M1. Production started late in 1942 and continued into 1944, with 16,000 units built.

The Tank Destroyer Force refused to place the towed 57-mm Gun M1 into service. The Army Ground Forces, however, did not seem bothered by the Tank Destroyer Force decision, and decided to make the 57-mm Gun M1 the standard towed antitank gun in U.S. Army infantry and armored divisions. By late 1943 it had completely replaced the towed 37-mm Gun M3A1. A 1943 infantry division was authorized 57 of the 57-mm antitank guns, while the armored infantry battalions of armored divisions, which rode into battle on M3 armored half-tracks, were authorized 30.

Even before D-Day, many officers and men of the Third Army's infantry divisions began to express doubts about the value of the 57-mm Gun M1 in combat. Patton addressed those concerns in May 1944 by stating his opinion on the matter in a letter of instruction to his corps and divisional commanders.

"There is a great lack of understanding about the use of the 57-mm antitank gun against tanks. These guns have a lethal range against tanks of approximately a thousand yards. Therefore, they must be emplaced in positions where they cannot see the enemy or be seen by him at ranges in excess of a thousand yards; otherwise they will be destroyed by shellfire before they become effective. The proper place for 57-mm antitank guns is on a reverse slopes or in positions where they can take the enemy under fire when he crosses the skyline or emerges from cover. When the 57-mm is used as accompanying artillery, and it should be so used unless enemy tanks are around, it follows the method of the cannon-company."

Pictured during the Battle of the Bulge in December 1944, the American crew of this 57-mm Antitank Gun M1 have seen heavy action, as indicated by empty mailing tube-type fiber ammunition containers, and shell cases in the foreground. During World War II the U.S. Army used moisture-resistant containers for practically all its ammunition except for "separate-loading projectiles," which did not require any outer packaging. *National Archives*

The Ordnance Department's efforts at trying to introduce a towed 90-mm antitank gun into service was delayed by design problems with the carriage and trails, and the fact that the Tank Destroyer Force could see no use for the large and heavy weapon. By the time the first production model appeared in December 1944, the effectiveness of large towed antitank guns had been discredited in the eyes of the Army's senior leadership by their poor showing in the early stages of the Battle of the Bulge. *National Archives*

The Tank Destroyer Force was stuck with a large inventory of towed antitank guns at its birth in 1942. Pictured in the early 1940s is an M2 armored half-track towing a 37-mm Gun M3A1 into the field during a training exercise in the United States. The M2 entered large-scale production in 1940. It was powered by White 160AX-gasoline engine that gave it a top road speed of 45 miles per hour. *National Archives*

As predicted by the Tank Destroyer Force, the 57-mm Gun M1 proved to be ineffective as a tank killer despite Patton's suggestions on its employment. It could be useful in limited secondary supporting roles, but it was viewed as excess baggage and was purposely lost on occasion by at least one of his armored divisions. Some of Patton's armored infantry battalions used the guns so infrequently that the crews were assigned to other duties.

The Ordnance Department also considered fielding a towed 76-mm and a towed 90-mm antitank gun during World War II. The war ended before the first 76-mm towed antitank gun was produced. Only 200 of the 90-mm towed antitank guns were assembled before the war ended. However, most of them had defective gun carriages and only one unit made it overseas before the war's end.

The Beginnings of the Tank Destroyer Force

A number of provisional antitank battalions were tested during the army's "war game" training in 1941. Their offensive role included vigorous reconnaissance, rapid movement to destroy enemy armored units before they could deploy, and the destruction of enemy armor with massed gunfire.

McNair, a strong supporter of a separate antitank force, had unconsciously adjusted the rules of engagement to favor the antitank units. The poor showing by the army's tank units, which attacked without infantry support, seemed to provide further evidence to prove the effectiveness of the provisional antitank battalions. The head of the Armored Force, Major General Jacob L. Devers, was not impressed by the antitank conclusions being drawn and summed up his feelings by stating: "We were licked by a set of umpire rules."

But Marshall pushed the concept and by August of 1941 the War Department was planning an enormous antitank program that would have committed over a quarter of the army's ground-fighting elements to highly mobile semi-independent antitank battalions.

Marshall and the War Department were supporting a doctrine that combat would soon show was fundamentally flawed. German tanks rarely attacked blindly or recklessly. Neither did they attack in the envisioned large numbers and all-tank formations. The British army had already learned in North Africa that the Germans closely integrated tanks, antitank guns, infantry, artillery, and aircraft into teams for both offense and defense. No other army before or during World War II would adopt the American doctrine of "pure" antitank warfare, preferring instead to simply increase the number and size of antitank guns at the divisional level or higher.

During an October 1941 meeting in Marshall's office, the new corps and field army level antitank battalions were renamed tank destroyer battalions because the term antitank was not aggressive enough for the new doctrine. The motto of the new tank destroyer force became "seek, strike, destroy," and an orange patch with a black panther chewing on a tank appeared on the shoulders of troop uniforms. Officers wore the new branch insignia—a half-track with an M1897 gun.

On November 27, 1941, the War Department ordered the activation of 53 tank destroyer battalions under the direct control of general headquarters (GHQ). This was followed in a few days by a further directive that transferred all existing antitank battalions from their parent units and placed them under GHQ control as well. Regimental antitank units remained at divisional level within U.S. Army infantry divisions.

These moves were not unanimously supported among army brass. In July 1940 Major General George A. Lynch, chief of infantry, advised the War Department "that the best antitank defense lies in the defeat of hostile armored forces by our own armored units." McNair quickly rebutted Lynch by stating his opposition to tank versus tank combat because such combat wasted tanks. He stressed that the tank's essential role was to go after unprotected personnel and material. McNair would write:

"Certainly, it is poor economy to use a $35,000 medium tank to destroy another tank when the job can be done by a gun costing a fraction as much. Thus, the friendly armored force is freed to attack a more proper target, the opposing force as a whole . . .."

The Merits of Towed Versus Self-Propelled Guns

One of the biggest problems for the newly formed tank destroyer force in early 1942 was the development and supply of the specialized weapons. Although self-propelled weapons were favored, most tank destroyer battalions at the time were using either trucks or armored half-tracks to tow 37-mm M3A1 or the 75-mm M1897A2 guns into action. Brigadier General Andrew D. Bruce, in

The crew of a 37-mm Gun M3A1 has deployed its weapon in a defensive position during a training exercise in the United States in the early 1940s. The complete weight of the gun and carriage was 3,400 pounds. Protection for the crew of the open-topped M2 towing vehicle seen in the background consisted of quarter-inch armor plates, which were bolted to the body framework. *National Archives*

Chapter Four   113

charge of the tank destroyer force, was a strong supporter of self-propelled weapons.

In Bruce's view, the ideal self-propelled tank destroyer would be a very simple design, light in weight, having high mobility, and armed with a 3-inch (76-mm) gun. McNair took the opposite position and insisted that self-propelled guns were too large to be concealed. He also implied that they would be unstable firing platforms, and less dependable and more expensive than the towed antitank guns. Marshall favored experimenting with self-propelled mounts.

The Ordnance Department proposed that the 3-inch antiaircraft gun designated the M3 be mounted on a small 8-ton full-tracked chassis known as the M5 Cletrac. Bruce detested all aspects of the weapon and referred it as the "cleak track" because it was slow, did not have enough armor protection, broke down almost constantly, and had a serious propensity to set itself on fire.

The Cleveland Tractor Company coined the name Cletrac. The chassis was based on an unarmored aircraft-towing tractor then being built by Cleveland Tractor. The Ordnance Department was so enamored with the Cletrac design that it got the War Department to standardize the vehicle as the M5 and approve the procurement of 1,580 vehicles on January 7, 1942.

The Ordnance Department's enthusiasm for the M5 Cletrac was dashed after a series of tests conducted at Aberdeen Proving Grounds in July 1942. These tests proved conclusively that the 12-ton vehicle was clearly unsuitable as a tank destroyer. An Ordnance Department observer described the condition of the vehicle after testing: "The sides were dished in, the gun supports buckled, the suspensions were out of line, the travel lock folded, and the gun mount loosened." After reviewing the test results, McNair admitted that the M5 looked "pretty hopeless" to Bruce.

Another vehicle considered for the role of self-propelled tank destroyer early on by the Ordnance Department was a six-wheeled armored car designed and built by Ford Motor Company. It featured an open-topped 360-degree rotating turret mounting a 37-mm gun. Before testing

The M5 Cletrac tank destroyer was powered by a six-cylinder Hercules diesel engine that gave it a top road-speed of 38 miles per hour and 20 miles per hour cross-country. Lacking a turret, the low-slung Cletrac, with its limited-traverse, forward-firing 3-inch gun, was only 5 feet tall. The vehicle had a length of 15 feet and a width of 8 feet 3 inches. The crew consisted of four men: vehicle commander, gunner, loader, and driver. *National Archives*

could begin it became clear that a gun more powerful was needed and the vehicle was passed over. However, the vehicle showed so much promise that the army took it into service and it became the standard armored car for cavalry reconnaissance units during World War II.

Since no weapon concepts remained to satisfy his needs, Bruce designed a weapon specifically for the tank destroyer role. The Gun Motor Carriage M18 had a five-man crew and was armed with a new 76-mm gun designated M1. The M18, also known by its unofficial nickname "Hellcat," had a low silhouette, excellent cross-country performance, and a top speed of over 50 miles per hour.

The M18 was by all accounts the perfect tank destroyer for the time. However, production of the vehicle would not begin until July 1943, and the first units did not reach the field until summer 1944. By that time, the M18's 76-mm gun had become unable to defeat late-war German armored fighting vehicles like the Panther and Tiger tanks.

Despite its firepower shortcomings, the high speed and unmatched mobility of the M18 earned the respect of crews who operated them in Western Europe. They were surprisingly effective against German tanks on some occasions. For example, on September 17, 1944, a tank-heavy German counterattack struck at a combat command of Patton's elite Fourth Armored Division at Arracourt, France. A platoon of four M18s belonging to the 704th Tank Destroyer Battalion destroyed 15 German tanks. The platoon lost three of its vehicles in a few hours of fighting, but the M18s came out on top.

Early Tank Destroyers

While waiting for the M18 to enter service, the Tank Destroyer Force used available weapon systems for both training and combat. The first of these stopgap weapon systems was the M3 Gun Motor Carriage (GMC) which entered the inventory in October 1941. It consisted of a modified version of the standard M3 armored half-track equipped with an

The Ford Motor T22 six-wheel armored car was originally intended as a candidate for the role of self-propelled tank destroyer in the U.S. Army. By the time it was tested in early 1942, it was already clear to all concerned that its turret-mounted 37-mm M6 gun was inadequate for the role intended. Rather than discard an otherwise well-designed vehicle, the army standardized it as the M8 Armored Car in June 1942. The M8 pictured belongs to the Virginia Museum of Military Vehicles. *Michael Green*

Chapter Four   **115**

The M18 Gun Motor Carriage (GMC) was 9 feet 2 inches tall, 17 feet 4 inches long, and 8 feet 5 inches wide. The suspension system utilized torsion bars, with five road wheels per side (each having a shock absorber) and four track return rollers. An adjustable dual-compensating wheel supported each steel track at the rear and provided a means of adjusting the track tension. The beautifully restored M18 pictured belongs to the vehicle collection of Frank Buck of Gettysburg, Pennsylvania. *Bob Fleming*

M1897A2 75-mm gun. The idea for this design came from the French, who had mounted their 75-mm gun on the bed of a five-ton truck.

The M3 GMC was common among U.S. Army tank destroyer battalions during early 1943. A pedestal mount with limited traverse supported the forward firing M1897A2 gun on the M3 GMC. A thin armor shield protected the gun crew from small arms fire. The army designated a later version with a modified gun mount as the M3A1 GMC.

Another early tank destroyer surrogate was the M6. The M6 was a light 3/4-ton Dodge 4x4 military truck carrying an M3A1 37-mm antitank gun on its rear cargo deck. The first prototype of the vehicle appeared in late 1941. The only armor on the vehicle was a thin-armored gun shield, protection against only light small arms fire. The gun could be traversed a full 360 degrees, but was usually fired to the rear, to the driver's relief.

Before the M6, the Ordnance Department had tried unsuccessfully to develop a jeep-mounted tank destroyer equipped with the M3A1

A rear three-quarter picture shows a second restored M18 GMC belonging to the vehicle collection of Frank Buck of Gettysburg, Pennsylvania. The M18 weighed in at 18 1/2 tons and was powered by a Continental R-975 C1 air-cooled radial gasoline engine giving it a top speed of 55 miles per hour on level ground. Located at the rear of the open-topped turret was a .50-caliber antiaircraft machine gun. *Bob Fleming*

Pictured at the Virginia Museum of Military Vehicles is an un-restored M18 GMC. In service, the vehicle had a five-man crew: a vehicle commander, gunner, loader, driver, and assistant driver. The first three worked in the open-topped 360-degree rotating turret. The driver and assistant driver rode in the left and right front of M18 hull. *Michael Green*

37-mm antitank gun. A number of experiments were conducted with rear-firing and forward-firing weapons mounted on jeeps. The Jeep chassis, however, was unable to handle the weight of a gun, gun crew, and ammunition.

A full-track armored chassis for the antitank weapon had been considered shortly after World War I but there was no follow-through. It was not until October 1936 that the infantry branch received authorization to build a prototype. A 47-mm antitank gun was installed in an open-topped turret mounted on an M2A1 light tank chassis. This self-propelled antitank gun performed so poorly in tests that the project was canceled in 1937.

In September 1941, the Ordnance Department proposed a full-track self-propelled weapon. The proposed chassis was the M3-series medium tank, which was then in full-scale production. As envisioned by the Ordnance Department, an M3 3-inch antiaircraft gun would be fitted on the open-topped superstructure in a limited-traverse, forward-firing position. Tests soon showed that

Two M3 75-mm GMCs have taken up defensive positions on the side of a paved road during a training exercise held in the United States during the early 1940s. The 75-mm gun was welded to a steel box behind the driver position. Nineteen rounds of ammunition were stored in racks located under the gun mount with another 40 rounds in bins under the floor behind the gun. *National Archives*

Chapter Four   **117**

Driving through a small American town during an early 1940 training exercise are a pair of U.S. Army M3 75-mm GMCs. The armor windshield plate in front of the driver's compartment was hinged to fold downward to allow greater depression of the weapon. The viewing ports in the armored windshield had internal adjustable sliding shutters to vary the view for the driver, depending on the threat from enemy fire. *National Archives*

The early efforts to develop a self-propelled mount for the U.S. Army's 37-mm Antitank Gun M3A1 involved mounting the weapon on a modified jeep chassis. Various configurations were tried with the weapon set up to either fire over the front or rear of the vehicle. Test results, as evident by this remarkable picture showing a 37-mm gun on a jeep at the moment of firing, showed the jeep frame could not take the recoil stresses, and the idea was dropped. *National Archives*

the large size and height of the prototype vehicle (designated T24) made it a better target than an antitank weapon.

However, the advantages of using a medium tank chassis to carry a large antitank gun were obvious. The Ordnance Department immediately proposed a new tank destroyer based on the modified chassis of the gasoline-powered M4A1 Sherman medium tank. An M7 3-inch gun (based on an old naval gun design) was mounted in an open-topped turret with full 360-degree traverse. The diesel-powered M4A2 replaced the M4A1 chassis prior to the start of production as the M10 GMC in September 1942. A Ford gasoline engine powered another version, the M10A1. Since M10 production was sufficient to meet the Tank Destroyer Forces needs overseas, the M10A1s were retained in the United States. Most were used as training vehicles or converted into armored recovery vehicles.

Bruce regarded the M10 as yet another stop-gap weapon system. It "weighs too much and is

118   Antitank Weapons

too slow." It also had a number of design faults, such as the lack of a power turret traverse. Bruce strongly opposed the continued development of the M10 and much preferred his M18.

By war's end the M10 would be the most numerous self-propelled tank destroyer in the army. The army had so many M10s at one point that at least one Army Ground Forces officer was quoted as saying: "We have more M10s than we know what to do with." The army had continued to build M10s throughout the war, even while it was reducing the number of self-propelled tank destroyer battalions.

The original Tank Destroyer Force plans called for the formation of 200 battalions. By early 1943 this number was revised downward to 144 battalions, but even this proved too many. The end of 1943 would find only 106 battalions activated. Of these 106 battalions, 61 saw action in Europe and 10 were sent to serve in the Pacific against the Japanese. The remaining 35 tank destroyer battalions were deactivated or were converted to other, more useful, purposes.

Lessons Learned

When President Roosevelt decided to commit American troops to the invasion of French North Africa in late 1942 the 601st and the 701st tank destroyer battalions were still equipped with the M3 GMC and the M6 GMC.

One military observer, referring to the M6, stated: "Sending such a patently inadequate destroyer into combat can at best be termed a tragic mistake."

Most of the M6s that arrived in North Africa were eventually stripped of their 37-mm guns and were used as ordinary trucks. Some of the M6s did see limited use in secondary roles as infantry support vehicles. A few resourceful American units in North Africa removed the 37-mm guns and mounted them on their M2 and M3 armored half-tracks.

Another serious problem confronting the tank destroyer battalions in North Africa was the continual failure of American commanders to adhere to the doctrine. Instead of keeping the tank destroyer battalions massed in the rear area to await

Due to the unsuitability of the jeep chassis as a self-propelled mount for the 37-mm Antitank Gun M1A1, the Ordnance Department began looking around for a larger vehicle capable of handling the recoil of the weapon. An early example of this line of development resulted in the crude mounting of a 37-mm gun on the Weapons Carrier version of Dodge's 1/2-ton 4x4 light truck. National Archives

Chapter Four 119

The M6 GMC consisted of a modified Dodge 3/4-ton 4x4 Weapon Carrier mounting a 37-mm Gun M3A1. The gun was placed on a steel pedestal in the rear cargo compartment of the vehicle giving it 360 traverse. In general practice the crew was taught the best firing position was to point the weapon rearward when engaging a target. A six-cylinder gasoline engine, giving it a top speed of 50 miles per hour on paved roads, powered the vehicle. *National Archives*

The pilot model of a 3-inch GMC mounted on the open-topped chassis of an M3 series medium tank. The vehicle was built by the Baldwin Locomotive Works and designated the T24. It was clear to all concerned that the vehicle was a design dead end, due to its high silhouette and lack of a 360-degree rotating turret. The M3 3-inch gun was removed in January 1942 and the vehicle returned to Baldwin. *National Archives*

an enemy tank attack, they were parceled out by companies to different infantry units. This pattern developed because the infantry's towed 37-mm M3A1 guns could not stop enemy tanks, one American military observer noted in a report:

Two general officers condemned this gun [the 37-mm M3A1] as useless as an antitank weapon and strongly recommended that it be discarded. They stated that it would not penetrate the turret or front of the German medium tank, that the projectiles bounced off like marbles, and the German tanks overran the gun positions.

While the reassignment of tank destroyer companies to infantry units did much to raise the morale of the ordinary soldier, it robbed the Tank Destroyer Force of the chance to prove the validity of its doctrine.

To better support infantry units, the tank destroyer units in North Africa were assigned missions suited to tank, reconnaissance, or artillery units. It soon became clear that when

Work done with the T24 and T40 convinced the Ordnance Department that a medium tank chassis armed with a 3-inch gun in a 360-degree rotating turret was a splendid idea. The Fisher Tank Division of General Motors completed a pilot model (as pictured) designated the T35 in April 1942. The T35 was based on the modified hull of a diesel-powered M4A2 Sherman medium tank. Notice the lack of a front hull-mounted machine gun. *National Archives*

After the Japanese attack on Pearl Harbor, it was decided to fit 50 older model M1918 3-inch antiaircraft guns on the open-topped chassis of the M3 series medium tank. The pilot vehicle was designated the T40. Having learned its lesson from the canceled T24 project, the Ordnance Department mounted the 3-inch gun much lower in the vehicle's superstructure, as seen in this March 1942 photograph. Like the T24, the project was a design dead end and canceled in August 1942. *National Archives*

Chapter Four 121

Work on the design plans for the T35 went ahead. Combat experience in the Philippines between American and Japanese ground forces stressed the advantage of sloped armor in deflecting antitank projectiles. The Tank Destroyer Force requested a second pilot model, to be designated the T35E1, of a possible full-track tank destroyer incorporating a lower silhouette and sloped armor plate. The armor arrangement on the T35E1 pilot vehicle is clearly seen in this picture. *National Archives*

The Ordnance Department was pleased with the test results of the T35E1 pilot vehicle, and after ordering a number of design changes, the vehicle was standardized as the 3-inch GMC M10 on June 4, 1942. Unhappiness with the poor ballistic properties of the cast turret on the T35E1 resulted in its replacement on the M10 with a welded armored turret. This nicely restored M10 belongs to the collection of the Virginia Museum of Military Vehicles. *Michael Green*

The 3-Inch Gun M5

The development of the towed 3-inch gun began in late 1941, when the Army Ground Forces decided it needed a new, more powerful antitank gun in service. The gun had to be able to destroy any known existing or future enemy tanks. Since time was of the essence, the Ordnance Department decided not to start from the ground up. Rather, it would utilize existing components to assemble a suitable candidate. The Ordnance Department therefore decided to take the barrel of the M3 antiaircraft gun and mate it with the breech mechanism, carriage and recoil system of the 105-mm M2 howitzer. The thrown-together weapon was standardized as the 3-inch Gun M5 on the carriage M1 in December 1941. This was done even before the Ordnance Department finished testing the new weapon. As can be expected, many defects were quickly uncovered during its service tests, mostly concerning the unsatisfactory carriage.

The Tank Destroyer Force was not interested in towed guns at the time and had future development of the 3-inch gun M5 canceled in the summer of 1942. The failure of the M5 Cletrac during its service tests caused the Army Ground Forces to overrule the Tank Destroyer Force and order the production of 500 examples of the 3-inch gun M5 on the M1 carriage on August 23, 1942.

Forced to work with the new towed 3-inch gun despite its dislike of the weapon, the Tank Destroyer Force, working together with the Ordnance Department, managed to correct many of its early design problems by coming up with a new carriage, designated the M6, in November 1943. The Army Ground Forces was so pleased that in February 1944 it commented: "The redesign of the 3-inch Gun Carriage M1 into the 3-inch Gun Carriage M6 has resulted in an excellent towed tank destroyer weapon." Combat experience would force the Army Ground Forces to reevaluate this statement by mid-1944.

The towed antitank gun decision was not recognized as a serious mistake until American ground units saw action against German late-war tanks in Western Europe. The large and unwieldy towed 3-inch Gun M5 on the M6 carriage lacked the mobility to keep up with other units or react to changing battlefield conditions. They were frequently overrun, causing a higher casualty rate than that of a comparable self-propelled unit. One tank destroyer officer commented on the superiority of self-propelled guns over towed guns:

"The appearance and knowledge that self-propelled tank destroyers were at hand was a major reason that the infantry attained success and victory. The towed guns can be just as brave and thoroughly trained, but they never give much 'oomph' to the fighting doughboy when the chips are really down."

During the Battle of the Bulge, most tank destroyer losses were in towed battalions. This was the final nail in the coffin for the towed antitank gun. By early 1945, the army's senior leadership acknowledged its mistake and started to convert tank destroyer battalions back to self-propelled guns.

Patton's instructions to his troops regarding the use of towed and self-propelled antitank guns were issued on March 6, 1944:

"Towed antitank guns should be well to the front and located to cover likely avenues of enemy tank approach. They must be emplaced so that they cannot see or be seen beyond their lethal antitank range. Self-propelled antitank weapons should be held in reserve to intervene against enemy armored attacks. They should locate routes to and firing positions from probable sites of future activities. All antitank guns should be trained to fire as artillery and be provided with a large proportion of high explosive shells."

these units undertook tanklike offensive operations they were at a terrible disadvantage against well-trained and better-equipped enemy forces. An American military observer in North Africa who witnessed several encounters stated: "The tank destroyer is definitely a defensive weapon. Wherever destroyers have bulged out on their own and tried to fight German tanks they have been knocked out."

One of the few successful tank destroyer actions during the Battle for North Africa was a defensive operation that occurred on March 23, 1943, near the town of El Geuttar in Northern Tunisia. Major General Terry Allen, commander of the U.S. Army's First Infantry Division, had gathered 31 M3 GMCs of the 601st Tank Destroyer Battalion together to defend his artillery units from a counterattack by the German army's 10th Panzer Division. During the ensuing engagement the Americans repulsed the enemy attack and destroyed 30 German tanks, for the loss of 21 M3 GMCs. Patton, however, refused to call the battle at El Geuttar a success, due to the very high losses suffered by the 601st Tank Destroyer Battalion.

By March 1943 M10s had started to replace M3s in the tank destroyer battalions sent to North Africa. The men of the Tank Destroyer Force were thrilled with the increase in firepower and cross-country mobility offered by the M10.

Despite the improved capabilities of the M10s, army senior leadership was beginning to agree with Patton's long-held belief that the only effective tank destroyer was another tank.

After observing tank destroyer battalions in action during the Sicilian campaign, Major General John L. Lucas wrote:

"The tank destroyer has, in my opinion, failed to prove its usefulness. I make this statement not only because of the result of this campaign but also after study of the campaign in Tunisia. I be-

Interior details of the M10 GMC can be seen in this cut-away view. Visible on the rear turret wall are a number of 3-inch rounds. In the rest of the vehicle, 58 main gun rounds were stored in circular, moisture-resistant containers on the inside of the hull, as seen in this drawing. Aside from the main gun rounds, there was also space on the vehicle for 300 rounds of .50-caliber machine gun ammunition. *National Archives*

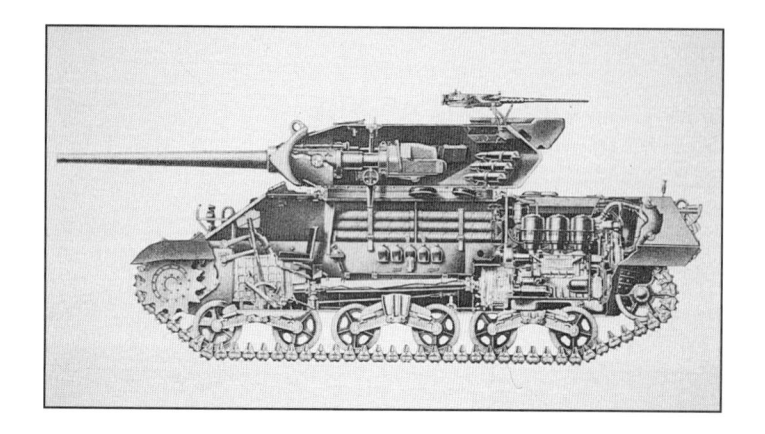

lieve that the doctrine of an offensive weapon to 'slug it out' with the tank is unsound."

General Omar Bradley, Patton's subordinate in North Africa, came away from the fighting convinced that towed antitank guns could be more effective than self-propelled antitank weapons. This belief was shaped by the very effective German employment of dug-in towed antitank guns in the wide-open spaces of North Africa. Many other high-ranking officers in the army shared Bradley's belief and soon commanded the Tank Destroyer Force to create a large number of towed battalions equipped with the 3-inch Gun M5. (The M5 was the same gun as mounted on the M10 Tank Destroyer with the only difference being the breech mechanism). Reluctantly, the Tank Destroyer Force rewrote its offensive-oriented doctrine to a defensive-oriented one.

More Bang for the Buck

Soon after the Allied invasion of France in June 1944, the Tank Destroyer Force faced the unpleasant reality that their weapons were ineffective in the role intended for them. Hastily arranged firing tests by the First Army on captured Panther tanks

The M10 GMC was lightly armored to keep its weight down. The upper front hull plate was only 1.5 inches thick. The gun shield on the M10 was the best-protected spot on the vehicle, with an armor thickness of 2.2-inches. The rest of the vehicle made do with an inch or less of armor plate. Some M10 crews decided to add a layer of cement-filled sandbags on the front hull plate for extra protection as seen in this World War II photograph. *National Archives*

124   Antitank Weapons

A number of M10s and M10A1s were supplied to the British army under land lease. In late 1944 the British began replacing the American 3-inch gun with their superior 17-pounder (76.2-mm) antitank gun. Rearmed, the vehicle was designated by the British as the "Achilles." To help balance the very long 17-pounder, a counterweight was fitted on the end of the barrel just behind the muzzle brake, as seen in this picture of an British Army Achilles at the moment of firing. *British Army Tank Museum*

Pictured at Aberdeen Proving Ground in November 1942 is the first pilot model of an M10 GMC fitted with a modified 90-mm M1 Antiaircraft Gun. The vehicle was designated the T7. Firing tests with the pilot vehicle went very well. The only problem that developed involved the slightly heavier 90-mm gun unbalancing the manually operated M10 turret. A decision was made to design a new and better-balanced turret with a power traverse mechanism. *National Archives*

Chapter Four   125

Due to the 5,850-pound weight of the 3-inch Gun M5, it needed a large truck to move it into or out of position, unlike self-propelled tank destroyers, which could maneuver for a flank shot at the weaker side armor of German heavy tanks. The M5 gun crew was normally confronted by the much thicker frontal armor of German tanks. *National Archives*

demonstrated that only shaped-charge rounds fired from the towed 90-mm antiaircraft gun and the 105-mm howitzer could penetrate the Panther's frontal armor. Even the 90-mm and 105-mm guns were useless against the thick well-sloped frontal armor of the German Tiger II tank.

Whenever possible, tank destroyer gun crews aimed for the sides or rears of Panther tank turrets or the opening through which their hull-mounted machine gun projected. American tank destroyer crews also discovered that rounds that hit the lower portion of a Panther tank's gun shield would ricochet downward and penetrate the vehicle's thinner top armor.

Sergeant Earnest B. Forster, in a World War II report, described the fate of M10 crews who could not hit the soft spots:

"While at Amperveiler I saw three dug-in tank destroyers with 3-inch naval guns open fire on two Mark V [Panthers] at a range of 800 yards, resulting in two ricochets on the German tanks and two tank destroyers knocked out, the third one withdrawing. The tank destroyer men held the element of surprise, but naval guns are not capable of knocking out the Mark V tank, unless at the proper angle."

The Ordnance Department was not taken completely by surprise when the M10 tank destroyers proved unable to destroy late-war German tanks. It had in early 1942 begun to plan for the appearance of more heavily armored enemy tanks by experimenting with mounting a modified 90-mm antiaircraft gun on a variety of full-tracked vehicles, including the M10.

The experimental mounting of a modified 90-mm antiaircraft gun in a turret of an M10 proved so successful that the Ordnance Department ordered two soft-steel pilot vehicles (designated T71) in early 1943. The Tank Destroyer

A key visual difference between the 3-inch GMC M10 and M10A1 and the new 90-mm GMC M36 was in the turret construction, as can be seen in this picture of an M10 parked in front of an M36. The M36 has a rounded cast-armor turret, as compared to the flat-sided welded-hull turret on the M10 and M10A1. The gun shield and the rear turret bustle on the M36 also differed in design from the earlier tank destroyer. *National Archives*

Belonging to the Virginia Museum of Military Vehicles is this unrestored 90-mm GMC M36. The rounded gun shield on the front of the turret was 3 inches thick. The turret walls were 1 1/4 inches thick all around. The rear turret bustle on the vehicle provided stowage space for 11 main gun ready rounds, out of a total of 47 carried in the vehicle. *Michael Green*

Chapter Four 127

Force objected to the program, stating: "The gun is not desired by the Tank Destroyers as a tank destroyer weapon, since it is believed that the 3-inch gun has sufficient power."

Overriding the shortsighted objections of the Tank Destroyer Force, the Army Ground Forces ordered the Ordnance Department to continue testing of the 90-mm weapon system. After much modification, including a brand new turret design, the T71 was approved for production in July 1944 as the 90-mm M36.

The Tank Destroyer Force was not alone in discounting the need for the M36. General Eisenhower, when asked in May 1944 if he wanted any 90-mm armed tank destroyers for the American forces slated for the invasion of Normandy, France, stated: "No T71s [M36s] are desired at this time for converting Bns [battalions] now under our control."

Eisenhower's advisors had told him that the existing 3-inch gun on the M10 or on the towed mount were able to defeat any German tanks encountered in France. Eisenhower, like other senior army officers, was also concerned about the needed retraining for the new weapon system so close to an invasion date. For this same reason, Eisenhower accepted only 40 of the M18 tank destroyers with 76-mm guns in March 1944.

Once Eisenhower became aware of the difficulty his men had in destroying German tanks, he sent a senior member of his staff to Washington to demand that the chief of staff of the army rush all available M36s to France. While Marshall ordered they be sent in July, the new tank destroyers did not arrive in Europe until September and October 1944.

Since the U.S. Army could not field a tank armed with a 90-mm gun with a sufficient level of

Guarding a street corner in the French City of Metz is a 90-mm GMC M36. On paper, the 90-mm gun on the M36 was suppose to penetrate 6 inches of armor at 1,000 yards. With two rounds, the gun could penetrate 5 feet of reinforced concrete. The rate of fire of the gun was a little slower than other GMCs because of the size and weight of the rounds. *National Archives*

128   Antitank Weapons

armor protection to engage in a fair fight with German tanks until the closing stages of the war in Europe, the M36 assumed the role of the army's main battle tank. The M36 was ill prepared for this role, with its very thin armor and lack of a hull-mounted or coaxial machine gun. The vehicle's open-topped turret was also a serious problem, since it left the gun crew exposed to hand grenades as well as artillery and mortar fragments.

Despite these shortcomings, the saving grace of the M36 was the ability of its 90-mm gun to destroy German tanks at 800 yards or closer. An example of this can be found in an extract from a World War II report that describes a single combat engagement:

"T/4 Brill, gunner, First Platoon of Company B, fired two rounds of 90-mm APC on December 25, 1944, near Calles, Belgium, into the front of Mark V [Panther] tank at a range of 200 yards. Both rounds penetrated the front slope plate and set the German afire."

At ranges over 800 yards, the situation for the crews of M36 tanks was entirely different, as can be seen in another extract from the same report.

"Lt. Clinton Brooks stated that at Gereonsweiler, Germany, on November 23, 1944, a Mark V [Panther] tank fired at the side of an M36, the No. 2 gun of his platoon, sending a round completely through the side. Lt. Brooks opened fire with the 90-mm at 3,000 yards firing a total of 20 rounds of which approximately half were APC. The German tank was hit many times but without damage. The M36 was forced to withdraw from the fire of the same tank."

As soon as the war ended, the army in Europe began to evaluate the effectiveness of its wartime operations. With the introduction of the heavily armored M26 Pershing heavy tank (later to be classified as a medium tank) mounting a 90-mm gun, tank destroyers like the M36 were clearly obsolete. The army soon took the logical next step and disbanded the Tank Destroyer Force once and for all.

Due to the high demand for the 90-mm GMC M36 in Western Europe, the Fisher Division of General Motors used the hulls of 187 M4A3 versions of the Sherman medium tank, in place of M10 or M10A1 hulls, to mount a 90-mm gun turret of the M36. With its hull stowage arrangements changed to accommodate the larger ammunition, the vehicle was designated the M36B1. *National Archives*

Chapter Four 129

Chapter Five

ANTIAIRCRAFT WEAPONS

World War I witnessed the birth of aerial warfare. In response to the new threat from the sky the various armies involved in the conflict developed a new piece of specialized equipment, the antiaircraft gun. The gun itself was nothing new. It was the gun mount that allowed the barrel to be aimed skyward at an elevation of up to 90 degrees that made it unique. The U.S. Army's senior leadership gave the job of air defense to the Coast Artillery Corps in 1917. This was done because it was the only part of the army that had practiced the art of firing at moving targets (ships).

It is important to remember that airplanes, unlike ground and seagoing equipment, operate freely in three dimensions. This made accurate firing of antiaircraft guns much more complex than equivalent surface to surface weapons.

To cope with the task of downing enemy aircraft, the U.S. Army's Coast Artillery Corps decided to modify two of its existing 3-inch seacoast defense guns for the antiaircraft role. One of the 3-inch guns was designated the AA Gun M1917. Due to its weight and power, it proved suitable only for static defense duties around U.S. Navy bases or civilian seaports. The other 3-inch gun was designated as the AA Gun 1918. Because it was lighter and less powerful than the AA Gun M1917, it was intended to be employed on a mobile trailer mount to accompany army units being sent to France. An order for 612 of the mobile AA Gun 1918 was placed in 1917, but none reached the field before the war ended.

Besides machine guns the U.S. Army had to depend on a small number of suitably modified French and British guns for

In World War I the various European armies often adapted existing field guns to the role of antiaircraft weapon. Since the field guns of the period had limited elevation, a number of methods were use to elevate the weapons to a proper firing angle. The Germans converted the 75-mm field gun pictured into an antiaircraft gun by mounting it on a wooden pestle that could be rotated 360 degrees. *National Archives*

the antiaircraft role during World War I. One of those was the vehicle-mounted French 75-mm Mle 1897 gun, nicknamed the "French 75." The gun was mounted on a rotating turntable with a platform for the gun crew on the rear deck of a truck. To steady the gun when firing, four outrigger arms fitted to the rear of the truck were deployed. The Allies, as well as the Germans, also developed a series of makeshift static mounts for defense of high-priority targets.

Despite the use of aircraft in the ground attack role during World War I, the senior leadership of the U.S. Army decided that air power was just a temporary fad that would have no lasting effect on the way it conducted combat operations. Compounding the army's general lack of interest in antiaircraft weapons was the fact that it was a stepchild of the coast artillery. Colonel E. Paul Semmens stated in his book *The Hammer of Hell* that by the 1930s, "Coastal artillery men were separated mentally and physically from the rest of the army ." They were not accepted partners in any combined arms plans under discussion or development by the army.

While future army officers in the 1920s and 1930s were instructed on the importance of defending forward combat units from potential aerial attack, most agreed with the Infantry School's 1933 statement that front-line units could provide most of the air defense themselves, without "special troops" (antiaircraft artillery). Besides, as was pointed out, coastal artillery personnel did not understand the way regular infantry units maneuvered and fought. The perception also existed at the time that coast defense officers and men generally lacked initiative.

Within such a hostile environment, recommendations by three successive coast artillery chiefs that antiaircraft units be permanently attached to the army's infantry divisions were

Most European armies realized even before World War I that they could never have enough static-mounted antiaircraft guns to defend every possible target. Rather, it made more sense to place a suitable antiaircraft gun on a wheeled vehicle that could travel to whatever area was most threatened by aerial attack. Pictured at the moment of firing is a truck-mounted British Army 13-pounder (3-inch) Mark 3 antiaircraft gun. The weapon could hit targets up to a ceiling of 17,000 feet. *National Archives*

The most easily adapted weapon in the inventory of European armies that could be put to work in the antiaircraft role was the machine gun. Pictured firing at an aerial target is an Italian soldier in France near the end of World War I. Despite their small-caliber ammunition and limited range, machine guns could be very effective against the slow and fragile low-flying aircraft of the time. *National Archives*

ignored. These prejudices were further strengthened by the most important single reality—lack of money. This meant that the development of expensive new air defense weapons was on "permanent hold."

In 1940 the U.S. Army finally approved the creation of separate antiaircraft battalions for attachment to its field divisions. Surprisingly, this event occurred over the strong objections of the Coast Artillery Corps, since it had changed its mind regarding the need for antiaircraft units. This last-minute change of heart reconfirmed to many in the army that the Coast Artillery Corps lacked first-class leadership. The Coast Artillery School contributed to this general impression within the army by not publishing a doctrine on the employment of separate antiaircraft battalions until late 1943. This resulted in continued confusion throughout the early part of the war, as each division, with an attached antiaircraft battalion, had to figure out how best to employ its antiaircraft assets in a tactical setting.

Improving Existing Antiaircraft Guns

Unable to acquire funding for new antiaircraft guns the Ordnance Department sought to improve the existing antiaircraft guns. With a new barrel design, the 3-inch AA Gun M1917 eventually became the M4 gun in 1928. It was placed on a static antiaircraft mount designated the M3. A small number of M4 guns on M3 static mounts were used to guard important locations in the Philippines and around the Panama Canal.

For field use, the Ordnance Department came up with a much-improved mobile 3-inch AA Gun M1918. The reworked weapon was standardized in 1927 as the 3-inch Antiaircraft gun M3. A suitable mount designated the M2 came into service the next year. The M2 was a pedestal mounting, nicknamed the "spider mount." It had four long outrigger legs over which a steel mesh platform was laid down for the gun crew in its firing position. For towing, the outrigger legs and the steel mesh platform of the M2 mount folded up into a compact mass. An improved version of the M2 mount was designated the M2A2 mount.

Shown in this picture taken in the 1930s is the U.S. Army's 3-inch M1917 Antiaircraft Gun on static-mount M4. Placing an antiaircraft gun on a static mount in the open had its advantages and disadvantages. The good points included 360-degree traverse and the ability to fire at high elevations. The downside was the lack of protection for the gun and crew from direct hits and strafing by enemy aircraft. *National Archives*

The crew of a coast artillery 3-inch M1917 Antiaircraft Gun is loading a fixed high-explosive round into the weapon's vertical sliding-wedge breechblock. To withstand the stresses of firing, sliding-wedge breechblocks tended to be very large and heavy. They were not used with guns firing separate-loading ammunition. *National Archives*

The crew of a 3-inch M1917 Antiaircraft Gun prepares to fire at an aerial target during a training exercise in the United States during the late 1930s. The aiming of antiaircraft guns like the 3-inch M1917 required a specially designed and constructed system of sighting and fire control equipment, to keep the piece continuously aimed on a target that could be changing azimuth, range, and altitude, all at the same time. *National Archives*

Emplaced for a firing mission during a 1930s training exercise is a U.S. Army 3-inch Antiaircraft Gun M1917. The optical instruments used in antiaircraft gunfire control devices presented a magnified image of the target to the observer's eye. Simultaneously, the observer also saw an image of a reticle, or reference mark, inside the instrument itself. By accurately superimposing the reticle image on the target image, the observer could establish an accurate aiming point to the target. *National Archives*

Chapter Five   **135**

Towed behind a truck in this picture taken in the 1930s is a U.S. Army 3-inch Antiaircraft Gun M1917. Most of the fire control work for an antiaircraft gun is done elsewhere than on the gun mount, but the gun mount does incorporate certain fire control gear, notably the sights. Sights are optical devices that can be used to position a weapon with respect to a straight line from the gun barrel to the target. *National Archives*

The M3 antiaircraft gun was a fairly effective weapon for use against military planes of the 1920s. It had a maximum effective ceiling of 31,200 feet. Unfortunately, it did not have the range to be effective against newer generations of fast high-flying military aircraft that began to appear in the 1930s. By 1933, the year Hitler and his Nazi Party came to power in Germany, the U.S. Army already knew the M3 antiaircraft gun was obsolete. Yet, like so many other weapons in the army inventory it would remain in service until the beginning stages of World War II.

Aircraft Warning Devices

In 1939 radar (originally an acronym made up of the words Radio Detection and Ranging) was still in it infancy and not yet in field use with antiaircraft units. To detect and locate hostile aircraft in darkness, coast artillery antiaircraft units employed powerful searchlights with up to 800,000,000 candlepower. Within the army, the searchlight units were affectionately called either "moonlight cavalry" or "smoothbore artillery."

Individual searchlights were mounted on lightweight four-wheel trailers towed by prime movers. Once emplaced, a searchlight was hooked up to a mobile power plant consisting of a gasoline engine that drove a direct current generator. Power from this unit was connected to the searchlight by two 200-foot cables. The plant also supplied power to an electric control system detector (manned by up to three operators) that guided the searchlight to its target. The effective range of searchlights on a clear night ranged between 8 and 10 miles.

In the field, searchlight batteries were normally arrayed in two concentric rings of light around antiaircraft batteries. The searchlights on the outer ring were the pickup lights, and those on the inner ring were the carry lights. For satisfactory gun battery operation, it was necessary to carry the target with at least two lights. Different conditions of visibility and attacks delivered at extremely high altitudes sometimes resulted in situations requiring three or more beams to "carry" a single target. The enemy target was normally carried until the target was destroyed; the target crossed the objective; or the target changed course, turned away from the objective, or passed beyond the extreme range of the searchlights and antiaircraft guns.

In 1939 coast artillery antiaircraft units still depended on primitive sound detection devices mounted on wheeled trailers to give advance warning of enemy aircraft flying at night. The first sound detection devices were put into service by the French during World War I, and consisted of nothing more than huge horns with a microphone fitted within. With these crude instruments trained listeners could tell the approximate direction from which enemy aircraft were approaching. This information would be passed onto the searchlight control system detector operators, who would point the searchlights in that direction to light up the incoming targets at the earliest moment possible.

On a reasonably quiet and calm night, the crew of a sound detection device could pick up a fairly noisy aircraft at a distance of 20 miles. A well-trained crew could also determine a good estimate of the aircraft's direction and altitude.

The first sound detection devices consisted of a single large horn. Later models, including those in use by the U.S. Army, had four horns, one pair funneling sound into the ears of the

Visible in this World War II-era picture is the crew of a General Electric searchlight M1941. The 60-inch mirror found within searchlights was parabolic in shape and reflected the light rays forward in an almost parallel pattern, producing a well-defined narrow beam of light. A ventilating fan mounted on top of the searchlight cooled and cleared the interior of the drum—which contained the mirror—of hot gases. *National Archives*

All the Army's prewar and wartime searchlights depended on the electric arc as their source of light. The arc was formed between two carbons, one known as the negative and the other the positive. The actual light source was an incandescent ball (globule) of vapor, formed in the high-intensity arc and held in a crater in the positive carbon. This globule of incandescent gas could be thought of as a miniature sun. *National Archives*

Chapter Five   137

Searchlights were aimed at aerial targets by use of the Control Station M1941, as pictured. The device consisted of a control unit and binocular mount placed on a tripod. The control station was connected to a searchlight by a 500-foot, 15-conductor cable. The control unit provided for the remote control of a searchlight in azimuth and in elevation. *National Archives*

Up until the very early days of World War II, U.S. Army antiaircraft units depended on the early warning of possible hostile aircraft with very large sound detection (binaural) devices, an example of which is seen in the left foreground of the picture. These devices were designed to work with searchlights by providing them the information on the general direction of approaching aircraft, a role later taken over by radar. *National Archives*

138   Antiaircraft Weapons

azimuth operator, the other pair serving the elevation operation. The last type of sound detection device in U.S. Army service before radar took over the role had only three horns.

British scientists, in June 1935, were the first to use radar to track an aircraft. Impressed by its military potential as an aircraft warning device, able to operate 24 hours a day effectively in almost any type of weather, the British government funded the construction of a chain of large static radar stations along its eastern coastline between 1935 and 1939. In early 1939 the German military constructed its own chain of 100 static early warning radar stations to guard the country's borders. During World War II both the British and the Germans developed a specialized form of radar system for aiming antiaircraft guns.

The U.S. Army Coast Artillery Branch began to press the army's top brass to spend money on the development of radar technology in early 1936. By May of that year the Signal Corps, which was assigned the responsibility for radar's

Deployed in the field during World War II is a U.S. Army SCR-268 radar unit designed for searchlight control. The word radar stands for radio detecting and ranging. Radar units themselves are fairly complex pieces of electronic equipment that send out radio waves, receiving echoes when the beam strikes an object. These echoes are converted into "pips" of light reflected on a tube face in such a manner that an operator can determine the identity, bearing, range, and the altitude of the object detected. *National Archives*

Well protected by a wall of sandbags is the towed van containing the crew and electronic heart of a U.S. Army SCR-584 gun-laying radar unit. Only the small radar dish of the unit is exposed, unlike the very broad unfocused beams generated by the SCR-268, which had a difficult time discriminating between targets flying close together. The narrow microwave beams sent out by the SCR-584 could automatically track an individual target and give very precise range, azimuth, and elevation data to a gun director, which aimed the guns of an aircraft battery. *National Archives*

Chapter Five   139

development in the U.S. Army, finished its first prototype. By 1940 production examples of the prototype radar system, now designated the SCR-268, were entering service. It was a mobile (trailer-mounted) system that had a maximum effective range of 24 miles and was designed to locate aircraft accurately enough that a coast artillery antiaircraft unit's searchlights would instantly pinpoint the plane. Dozens of SCR-268 radar sets were deployed with U.S. Army units in the battle for North Africa (1942–1943), where they proved effective in many situations. They also were very vulnerable to jamming.

With the limited success of the SCR-268, the next step was the development of a mobile (trailer-mounted) radar system not so easily jammed that could aim the guns of an antiaircraft unit directly, without searchlights. Such a system is known in military terminology as a gun-laying radar. A gun-laying radar must be able to determine range, azimuth (compass direction), and elevation of a target with high precision to achieve effective gunfire.

The army's first production example of a new gun-laying radar, designated the SCR-584, appeared for testing in May 1943. It did well in tests and was rushed into service. The SCR-584's first combat use occurred during the fighting for the Anizo beachhead in Italy in early 1944, where it enabled gunners to play havoc with the aerial attacks by the German Luftwaffe.

The SCR-584 provided antiaircraft units with the automatic tracking of both high and low-flying aircraft out to 27 miles, with an early warning range of 56 miles. The combat effectiveness of the SCR-584 soon won excellent reviews, and it was in widespread demand throughout the remainder of the war.

The army's short-range SCR-584 gun-laying radar units were tied in with the army's mobile SCR-270 long-range (110 miles on average) air search (surveillance) radar units whenever possible. (Air search radar is called a two-coordinate system since it measures only range and bearing). It was a brand-new army SCR-270 air search radar unit installed

A crewman on a U.S. Army 90-mm antiaircraft gun M1 is pictured loading a 23.4-pound high-explosive round into the weapon's sliding-wedge breechblock. The projectile left the barrel with a muzzle velocity of 2,700 feet per second. The maximum ceiling for the weapon was 39,500 feet. The combination of gun and mount together weighed in at 32,300 pounds, requiring a 6x6 truck for towing purposes. *National Archives*

in Hawaii that first detected incoming Japanese naval aircraft on the morning of December 7, 1941. The SCR-270 would serve alongside the SCR-268s in North Africa with Patton's forces, as well as in Sicily, and later in Western Europe.

Upgrading the Army Antiaircraft Weapons

During the Spanish Civil War (1936–1939) the Germans, Italians and Soviet armies used Spain as a training ground to test new types of weapons and tactics. Nervous American military leaders and politicians began to call for improvements to the U.S. Army antiaircraft weapon systems. By the late 1930s public pressure also began to demand improvements in the army's weapons and equipment. Funding appropriations for modernizing the coast artillery's antiaircraft weapons was greatly increased over those of previous years.

The coast artillery's excitement on receiving funding for new and long-awaited antiaircraft weapons was tempered during the 1930s, because the War Department had continued to reject the coast artillery's recommendation that antiaircraft units be permanently attached to front-line combat units. The War Department believed the only air defense requirement it could envision was centered on protecting the army's rear area positions from high-flying enemy bombers. For this reason the budgetary increases allotted to the Coast Artillery Corps of the late 1930s were aimed at the development of a new, more powerful antiaircraft gun to replace the obsolete 3-inch M3 antiaircraft gun.

To come up with a new antiaircraft gun quickly, the Ordnance Department rushed the development of a 90-mm gun first proposed in 1938. The selection of that caliber had been determined by the weight of a shell that could be hand

A device known as a director, an example of which is shown, controlled the aiming and the firing of large-caliber antiaircraft guns in all armies during World War II. A director was normally manned by five men: a control officer, pointer, trainer, radar operator, and range finder operator. The pointer and trainer kept the director's line of sight on target in optical tracking. Each had a firing key that could be selected to control the firing circuit, although the pointer was most often in control of firing the guns. *National Archives*

Pictured somewhere in the Pacific theater of operations during World War II is the four-man crew of a U.S. Army M1 Optical Height Finder. It formed part of the fire control system of the Army's 90-mm antiaircraft gun batteries. The soldier standing in front of the M1 is the altitude setter. The three soldiers located behind the M1 include the elevation tracker on the far right of the picture, the stereoscopic observer in the center, and the azimuth tracker on the far left of the picture. *National Archives*

loaded; anything more than 40 pounds for a complete round would be too heavy for gun crews to handle for more than a few minutes at a time. This design consideration was forced upon the army because a reliable mechanical loading system had not yet been developed.

In late 1939 and early 1940 the Ordnance Department decided to make several changes in the original design of its new antiaircraft gun. A series of brief tests confirmed that the modifications made seemed to work well, and gun and mount were standardized in February 1940 as the 90-mm Gun M1.

Shortly after the introduction of the M1 version of the 90-mm antiaircraft gun began, an improved version designated the M1A1 appeared with a spring-operated shell rammer. The new shell rammer was not a success in service since it had a habit of occasionally mashing fingers.

Gun crews were also convinced that they could load their weapon faster by hand and often turned the device off.

The original design of the 90-mm Gun M1 lacked automatic control, meaning the weapon's large and heavy 15-foot barrel was traversed and elevated by manual effort. When confronted by high-speed aircraft, hand tracking and aiming led to a very low hit probability. Consequently, the Ordnance Department added the servo-operated M2 remote control system to the M1A1 version of the 90-mm antiaircraft gun. This feature brought the rate of fire up to 27 rounds per minute.

A remote control system (as used during World War II by a U.S. Army 90-mm antiaircraft battery) was a combination of electrical and hydraulic controls. These controls received electrical guidance from M9A1 directors, primitive analog computers with attached telescopes that continuously provided the mathematical solutions predicting the flight paths of aircraft and furnishing fuse settings for multiple antiaircraft guns).

The director sent information to individual guns of a battery by means of dial settings. The gun crews merely matched dial pointers on their guns with the pointers of the director. As the gun crews moved their pointers, the gun moved with it. One member of the gun crew set the elevation, another set gun azimuths (compass directions), and the third set fuse ranges. These settings were constantly changed as a target moved so that the gun was always aimed at the correct location.

While the M9A1 director calculated the position of an enemy aircraft and how long it would take a shell to travel from gun to target. That device was a large 13.5-foot-long stereoscopic optical height finder (M1A1) that continuously determined the slant range and altitude of aircraft targets in clear weather, daylight conditions. (There are two types of ranges, horizontal and slant. Horizontal range is self-explanatory. The slant range is measured along the line of sight from ground position to an aerial target.)

The M1A1 height finder operated on the stereoscopic principle of merging the two slightly dissimilar target images transmitted to each eye into a single image, which was aligned in depth with a stereoscopic reticle pattern. (A reticle is a reference mark or pattern in an optical system, visible to the user of the system). Data read on the range-height scale were electrically transmitted to the M9A1 director.

For inclement weather conditions or darkness, a height-finding radar unit designated the SCR-547 was placed into U.S. Army service during World War II. The M1A1 optical height finder was retained as a backup system in units equipped with the SCR-547.

As a last resort, aiming the M1A1 version of the 90-mm antiaircraft gun at an enemy plane could be accomplished by using the direct-fire sighting instruments on the gun mount.

Improving the 90-mm Antiaircraft Gun

The haste with which the army placed the 90-mm Gun M1 into service left insufficient time to put the weapon through field and maneuver tests that might have exposed a number of unforeseen design shortcomings. These shortcomings including both the spring-operated shell rammer and a two-wheel, single-axle carriage that proved difficult to tow across rough terrain. Another problem was the time-consuming process needed to prepare the gun for firing. The fighting in North Africa in early 1943 highlighted these problems to all concerned.

Successful German use of their towed 88-mm antiaircraft gun in the antitank role during the fighting in North Africa made a strong impression on the senior leadership of the American army. It was decided to make some important changes to the 90-mm Gun M1 and M1A1 versions. The original design of the guns did not allow it to fire at targets below the horizon, a key requirement in the antitank role. A redesigned 90-mm gun designated the M2 (fielded in late 1943) corrected the design shortcoming by permitting the gun to be depressed below the horizon. Another important design feature of the M2 was a much-improved two-axle trailer that was easier to tow and to emplace into a firing position.

To replace the unsatisfactory spring shell-rammer on the M1A1 the army accepted into service

Fuses

The standard large antiaircraft round (75-mm and up) employed during World War II was a high-explosive shell set to explode with the aid of a mechanical, spring-activated timefuse. Typically these rounds would have an effective bursting radius of 35 to 50 yards. Individual military aircraft that changed altitude rapidly while being fired upon by antiaircraft guns equipped with time fuses could generally avoid destruction. Multiengine bombers flying in formation needed to maintain both the same speed and altitude to maximize the accuracy of their bomb runs and were therefore much more vulnerable to time fuses.

A fuse is intended not only to explode a shell's main charge (referred to as the burster charge) at the right time; it is also intended to prevent explosion at the wrong time. A fuse is "armed" when it is made ready to function.

Late in World War II, U.S. Army antiaircraft and artillery units began using proximity fuses. These fuses are miniature radio transmitters and receivers, powered by tiny battery cells. When the projectile approaches closely to a target, the radio waves sent out by the transmitter are reflected back to the receiver in sufficient strength to close a circuit that initiates fuse action. This advancement in technology dramatically improved the effectiveness of the army's antiaircraft units for the remainder of the war in Europe. Patton was quoted during the Battle of the Bulge as stating: "I think that when all armies get this shell, we will have to devise some new method of warfare."

Due to the obvious limitations of optical height finders, the U.S. Army fielded the SCR-547 radar unit during World War II. The appearance of the identical radar dishes led to its popular nickname, the "Mickey Mouse." Height-finding radar units are three-coordinate systems. They are capable of discriminating between targets that are close together, and they are capable of measuring range, bearing, and altitude. *National Archives*

Pictured at the moment of firing, with the barrel in full recoil, is a U.S. Army 90-mm Antiaircraft Gun M2. The M2, unlike the earlier M1 and M1A1 versions, was mounted on its carriage so it could be fired at ground and sea targets as well as aerial targets. This increase in capability earned the weapon the nickname as the "triple threat." *National Archives*

the M20 electrically controlled fuse setter-shell rammer. The M20 was an ingenious device that slowly fed a complete round of ammunition into rotating rubber rollers set into the breech ring that drew the round into the fuse setter jaws. There, it stopped until the jaws received the aircraft position signal from the director. Then the jaws rotated the time fuse to explode at the correct altitude. Thereupon the jaws opened and the round was automatically rammed into the breech, the breech closed, and the round was fired. This decreased the dead time between manually setting the fuse and the moment of firing. As a fast-flying plane could move a considerable distance in that interval, use of the M20 greatly improved accuracy for the M2 version of the 90-mm antiaircraft gun.

Other improvements to the M2 included the addition of the M12 remote control system, which operated on the same principle as the earlier M2 remote control system. The only difference was

In a picture taken in North Africa during World War II, a U.S. Army 90-mm Antiaircraft Gun M1 stands in front of a captured German 88-mm antiaircraft gun. At the foot of the carriage of the American weapon is the unsatisfactory two-wheel single-axle carriage that caused the Army so much unhappiness in North Africa. To provide the crew of 88-mm guns some limited protection from small arms fire when engaged in ground support operations, the Germans designed a thin armored shield that was added to the weapon's carriage. *National Archives*

that it was connected with a newly developed electrical off-carriage director, instead of the earlier mechanical director found with the M1A1 version of the 90-mm antiaircraft gun.

Antiaircraft Machine Guns

The successful German invasions of Poland in 1939 and France in 1940 forced the U.S. Army to reevaluate its belief that front-line combat units did not need protection from enemy aircraft. What brought home this point was the American observation of the important role that ground support aircraft played in German offensive operations. German doctrine called for air attacks to rupture defensive lines in the way that artillery had done in earlier wars. German ground-attack aircraft were normally used to attack enemy command and control centers and logistics depots. To assist in the coordination of the air and ground units, German Air Force (Luftwaffe) liaison officers were attached at the divisional level of the German army.

The effective employment of highly mobile divisional level antiaircraft units within the German army also caught the attention of many American military officers. Despite the objections of some within the U.S. Army, it was decided that an urgent need existed for large numbers of fast-firing (automatic) short-range antiaircraft weapons to defend against low-flying planes. These weapons were to complement the 90-mm Gun M1. The weapon chosen for this task was the Browning .50-caliber machine gun.

Of the two types of .50-caliber machine guns available for use as antiaircraft machine guns by the Coast Artillery Corps (air-cooled and water-cooled) the preferred choice was the water-cooled version. Because a dependable source of water may not always be possible under combat conditions, an air-cooled heavy-barreled (HB) model was also designed for ground use where long bursts of fire might be necessary. The added amount of metal in the barrel of the machine gun absorbed heat just as water-cooling dissipated it.

To increase the muzzle velocity and accuracy of both the air and water-cooled .50-caliber machine guns, and to reduce flash and smoke, the

Chapter Five 145

Lessons learned from studying captured German 88-mm antiaircraft guns convinced the U.S. Army of the benefits of providing its 90-mm antiaircraft gun personnel a basic level of armored protection. The result of that decision can be seen in this official Ordnance Department photo showing an M2 version of the 90-mm antiaircraft gun with armored shield fitted on either side of the gun barrel. *National Archives*

Pictured at the U.S. Army Desert Training Center, sometime in the early 1940s, is the three-man crew of a water-cooled version of the .50-caliber M2 machine gun. On the right side of the weapon's receiver is a long canvas bag designed to catch the ejected links. The gun was 66 inches long and weighed 100 pounds. Another 21 pounds of water was in the metal jacket that encircled the gun's barrel. The maximum effective range was 2,500 yards. *National Archives*

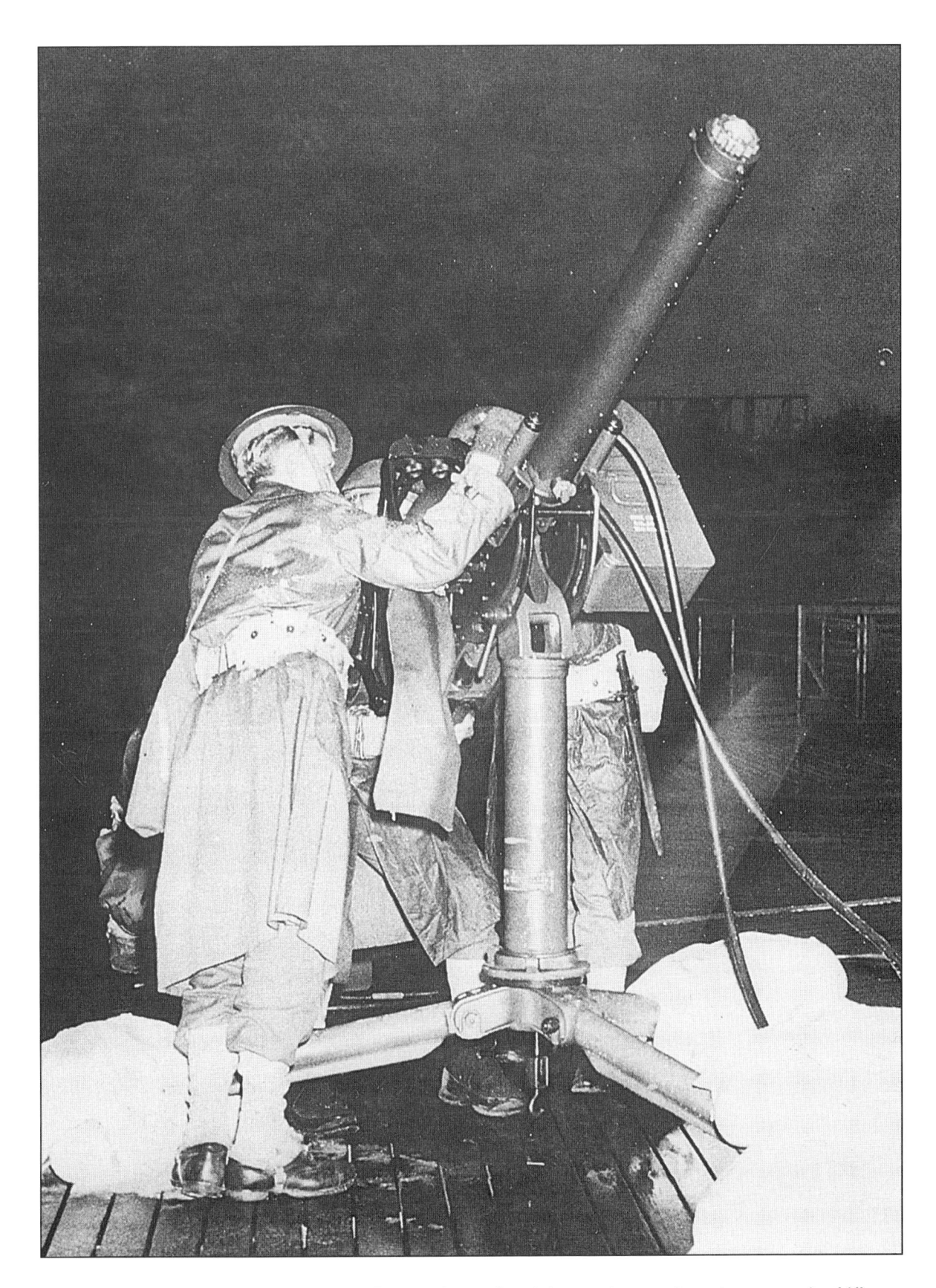

U.S. Army soldiers aim their water-cooled version of the .50-caliber M2 machine gun skywards during a nighttime rain shower. There were a number of different mounts developed for use with the Army's .50-caliber machine guns. The most common in the antiaircraft role was the large M3 tripod mount as pictured. It weighed over 300 pounds and provided a fairly stable firing platform. An armored shield could also be added to the M3 mount if needed. *National Archives*

Chapter Five   147

barrel was lengthened on both models from 36 to 45 inches. Early models of the air-cooled .50-caliber machine gun could fire 400 to 500 rounds a minute, while the water-cooled model could fire 500 to 650 rounds per minute. Early in the war, the rate on both types was pushed about 50 rounds a minute higher. In the last months of the war, an experimental barrel lightened from 28 to 20 pounds permitted considerably faster rates of fire. However, by that time the danger from low-flying enemy aircraft had almost disappeared. The army therefore concluded that the added wear on the barrel was too great to warrant a .50-caliber machine gun with a faster rate of fire.

If .50-caliber antiaircraft machine guns themselves required few changes after 1940, their mounts were another story. The original tripod mount adopted in the 1930s was quickly deemed too heavy (500 pounds), too hard to transport, and having insufficient elevation to be suited to close-in defense against low-flying, high-speed targets. A new .50-caliber mount capable of being transported in and fired from the army's jeep or 1 1/2-ton trucks was badly needed.

Upon the basis of two designs prepared by Rock Island Arsenal, the Heintz Manufacturing Company of Philadelphia built an acceptable model that was standardized in 1942 by the army as the M3. The new mount weighed 380 pounds, including the armored shield for the gunner. It also had the desired elevation of 15 to 90 degrees, and a simple ring sight.

Early in 1943, before the new .50-caliber M3's mounts became available in sufficient numbers, the Ordnance Department developed a stopgap cradle device, designated the Elevator Cradle M1, that could be affixed to heavy-barreled .50-caliber machine gun tripod mounts. The newly developed device allowed .50-caliber machine gunners enough elevation with their weapons to engage low-flying enemy aircraft. The makeshift cradle was standardized in August 1943 as the Elevator Cradle M1, with 80,000 put into service before the summer of 1944. They

The U.S. Army crew of a .50-caliber air-cooled M2 machine gun aim their weapon at an imaginary target for the benefit of the photographer. The weapon pictured is a very early production example of the M2, with a 36-inch barrel. Beginning in 1938 the Army began phasing into service a new 45-inch barrel for the M2. The added length improved the weapon's muzzle velocity, meaning each round packed more punch when it struck a target. *National Archives*

Attempts at improving the mobility of the U.S. Army's smaller antiaircraft guns resulted in a number of experiments in the early 1940s. These experiments were aimed at mounting water-cooled M2 .50-caliber machine guns on the rear cargo bays of various types of trucks. Due to the top-heavy weight of the weapon on its M3 tripod mount the arrangement shown was only intended to prove the premise and not as a practical solution to the concept. *National Archives*

performed a crucial role in supplementing the supply of antiaircraft mounts at a time when strafing enemy planes were a threat in every theater of operations.

Meanwhile, the Airborne Command requested mounts that could be put into action faster than the standard M3. A search began in 1943 for a suitable candidate. It had to weigh less than 160 pounds, be transportable by two men, and possess good firing stability. The search culminated in May 1944 with a satisfactory model designated the M63. The M63 was based on a Heintz Manufacturing Company design, modified by a quadruped base with horizontal legs and a folding, T-shaped trigger extension attached to the cradle. It weighed only 144 pounds. Nearly 48,000 were produced before the end of the war and they filled the need for mounts that could be airborne, landed from small boats, or carried into places inaccessible to vehicles.

Multiple Machine Gun Mounts

The army had recognized early in the war that fire aimed at low-flying enemy aircraft could be increased not only by more rapid rates of fire from individual guns, but also multiplying guns trained upon a target by a single gunner. This soon led to the development and use of multiple mountings for air-cooled .50-caliber machine guns.

As early as 1929, the Ordnance Department began thinking about mounting multiple .50-caliber machine guns on wheeled vehicles as a highly mobile antiaircraft vehicles. Tests with a variety of truck types proved unsatisfactory, and lack of interest by the Coast Artillery Corps effectively ended the project.

By 1940 the Coast Artillery Corps decided that truck or armored half-track mounted .50-caliber machine guns were not such a bad idea. The Ordnance Department again set about finding the right combination of vehicle and machine

The crew of a U.S. Army M13 Multiple Gun Motor Carriage waits under a camouflaged net for the approach of hostile aircraft during the Battle of the Bulge. The two-gun power-driven turret on the M13 could be traversed 360 degrees in six seconds. The guns could be depressed to minus 10 degrees or raised to 90 degrees elevation in less than two seconds. *National Archives*

gun mount. The Maxson Company submitted an electrically powered twin .50-caliber machine gun turret consisting of an elevating mechanism mounted on a turntable. Tests proved that the design was sound, and it was soon standardized as the Twin Caliber .50 Machine Gun Mount M33.

Of all the vehicles tested with the M33 Mount, the M2 armored half-track proved the most suitable. The army soon approved the design and ordered the combination into production using the slightly longer M3 armored half-track instead of the M2. The new antiaircraft vehicle was designated the Multiple Gun Motor Carriage M13 in July 1942. A total of 1,103 of the M13 were accepted into army service between January and May 1943.

The Ordnance Department's success with the M13 encouraged it to take the next step and come up with a slightly modified Maxson turret to carry four .50-caliber machine guns. Development of the project began in April 1942 and resulted in the production of a modified turret designated the Multiple Caliber .50 Machine Gun Mount M45. The M3 half-track with the M45 Mount fitted was designated as the Multiple Gun Motor Carriage M16. Production of the M16 started in May 1943 and lasted until almost the end of 1944 with 3,618 units completed. The total included conversions of some of the M13 armored half-tracks mounting the original M33 turret, as well as a small number of experimental M3 half-tracks armed with twin 20-mm Oerlikon guns designated the T10. The T10 never went into production because testing showed the guns jammed easily in dusty conditions. The 20-mm Oerlikon gun was much more successful as a ship-mounted antiaircraft gun and saw widespread use by the U.S. Navy during World War II.

The army's infantry divisions depended on a trailer-mounted version of the M45 Mount to protect them from low-flying enemy aircraft. It was designated the Multiple Caliber .50-Machine Gun Carriage M51 and could be towed into action by light trucks. Some army units in Europe preferred the superior mobility of a half-track mounted quad .50 caliber mount and converted

To provide the maximum field of fire for the crew of the four-gun M16 Multiple Gun Motor Carriage, and its predecessor, the two-gun M13, the vehicles were designed to have the upper portions of their rear compartment armored plates fold downward, as can be seen in this picture. The vehicle gunner sat in a small open-topped armor enclosure located between the guns. Ammunition for the guns was fed from quick-change drums, also seen in this photograph. *National Archives*

a number of towed M45 Mounts to fit on standard M2 and M3 half-tracks.

In 1943 a variation of this M51 carriage was designed for airborne use. To fit inside the gliders and transport planes used by the airborne forces, it was made much smaller and lighter by fitting the armored gun mount on a two-wheel trailer. Lacking the stability of a four-wheel trailer, the airborne version of the M51 was fitted with mechanical jacks permitting rapid emplacement and leveling for firing, once the trailer wheels had been removed. It had special armor shield and a handlebar control for turret movement and firing.

Combination Antiaircraft Gun Mounts

In September 1941, at the request of the Coast Artillery Corps, the Ordnance Department began development of a combination antiaircraft mount designated the M42. The mount consisted of a single 37-mm antiaircraft gun and two water-cooled .50-caliber machine guns on an M2 half-track. It was intended that tracer fire from the machine guns would assist the gun crew in aiming the larger and more powerful 37-mm gun. Tests with early prototypes of this weapon system, designated the T28, were not judged successful, since the heavy recoil of the 37-mm gun imposed an undue strain on the vehicle chassis.

The T28 project officially ended in April 1941, but was not forgotten.

When President Roosevelt made the decision to invade French North Africa in late 1942, the army saw a desperate need for additional antiaircraft vehicles. It was decided in June 1942 to restart the T28 project. To improve the design, the Ordnance Department placed the gun mount on an M3 half-track. The new vehicle was designated the T28E1 Combination Gun Motor Carriage. Because of a lack of time, little of the normal testing process was completed. Instead, the T28E1, now standardized as the M15 Combination Gun Motor Carriage, was rushed into production with 80 vehicles built between July and August 1942. These vehicles soon proved their effectiveness, as seen in this official army report from the fighting in North Africa:

"The proficiency of this mobile weapon can be attributed to three characteristics: its mobility, enabling it to work well in close support of combat troops in forward areas and to patrol roads over which heavy traffic must travel under constant threat of bombing and strafing; its flexible firepower, combining the volume of caliber .50 with the knocking power of the 37-mm; and the facility which its fire is controlled, by using the tracer stream of one caliber .50 to bring it on the target before opening with the full volume of its armament. Numerous cases are cited in which a 'mouse trap' effect has been obtained when enemy planes came in much closer on the initial caliber .50 fire than they would on light cannon and are caught by the 37-mm."

The success of the M15 encouraged the army to order another 600 of the weapon systems. These were built between February 1943 and April 1943. Unlike the first 80 examples of the M15, which were sent into combat without armored gun shields, the 600 follow-on vehicles had armored shields fitted. Unfortunately the extra armor badly overloaded the M3 half-track chassis and caused problems with its performance and mechanical reliability.

In an effort to correct the various shortcomings discovered in the M15 design, the Ordnance Department came up with a new lighter and improved gun mount designated the M54. It placed less of a strain on the M3 half-track chassis than the earlier gun mount. In place of the water-cooled .50-caliber machine guns, the M54 mount featured two air-cooled .50-caliber machine guns.

The first generation M42 gun mounts were soon replaced on a one-to-one basis with the new M54 gun mount. In this new configuration the rebuilt vehicles were standardized as the M15A1 Combination Gun Motor Carriage in August 1943.

Patton described in a letter of instruction (dated April 3, 1944) to some of the officers of the Third Army how the various self-propelled and towed antiaircraft guns should be employed in battle:

"At least one, preferably self-propelled, AA weapon should be attached to each company or battery of artillery, infantry, or tanks. There should be two at headquarters from the division up. The 155 and larger guns should have at least the AA mounts (static) per battery. Owing to our air superiority, AA should never open fire until attacked. AA is also good for antitank."

37-mm Antiaircraft Gun

After World War I the army recognized the need to develop an automatic 37-mm antiaircraft gun to fill the gap between the short-range machine guns and the larger antiaircraft guns designed to hit high-flying bombers. While the various ver-

A German soldier inspects a captured U.S. Army trailer mounting the same four-gun power-operated armored turret found on the M16 Multiple Gun Motor Carriage. In U.S. Army service the combination was designated the Multiple Caliber .50 Machine Gun Mount M45. *National Archives*

A battery of U.S. Army M1A1 37-mm antiaircraft guns stands watch for enemy planes. The wheeled mount and gun weighed 6,125 pounds and were towed into action by a light truck. The weapon fired a 1.34-pound high-explosive projectile at a muzzle velocity of 2,600 feet per second. The maximum ceiling was 18,600 feet. Visible in the picture are the two open ring sights used to aim the gun manually. *National Archives*

sions of the army's .50-caliber machine gun, in single or multiple mounts, could be very effective in the antiaircraft role they did have some serious limitations, including their relatively short range, their typical dependence on the human eye for aiming, and lack of knockdown power.

A key advantage of fielding a 37-mm antiaircraft gun was the size of the projectiles they fired. Due to their far greater mass, they could destroy a target that machine gun bullets might hit without seriously damaging. Unlike the larger shells fired from the 90-mm antiaircraft gun, equipped with time fuses, midrange antiaircraft such as the proposed 37-mm were designed to fire a supersensitive impact fuse that would explode on contact with any portion of an aircraft. A self-destruct device would detonate the shell if it missed its target and began to fall back to earth.

American weapon designer John M. Browning came up with a design for a 37-mm automatic gun in 1921. The Ordnance Department initially saw Browning's design as possibly filling the role of infantry cannon as well as an antiaircraft gun. With Browning's assistance until his death in 1926 and later with the help of the Colt's Patent Fire Arms Company, the Ordnance Department continued working on the design. Eventually, a model of the gun was standardized in 1927.

The Ordnance Department recognized that Browning's 37-mm gun was unsuitable as an infantry gun after field tests conducted in 1932. Work, however, continued on converting the gun into an antiaircraft gun. Two government arsenals were tasked with developing a satisfactory sighting device (known as a gyroscopic lead-computing sight) for the 37-mm gun, now designated the M1A2. A carriage designated the M3 was finally approved for production in 1938. Development of a satisfactory sighting system proved more elusive.

Chapter Five

With the threat of another world war growing more likely in 1938, the Ordnance Department decided to overlook the design shortcomings of the 37-mm antiaircraft gun and order it into production. As with so many other weapons prematurely rushed into service, the Ordnance Department spent the next few years trying to make the weapon fit for service as problems cropped up in the field.

One of the numerous modifications made to the 37-mm antiaircraft gun involved lowering the weapon's muzzle velocity to prevent premature bursts from new self-destroying tracer ammunition. Lowering the gun's muzzle velocity also lessened barrel erosion. The unsatisfactory American-designed sighting system was scrapped for a British-developed system designed for a 40-mm antiaircraft gun. The British system consisted of a remote control system mounted on the carriages of the 37-mm antiaircraft guns and linked to an off-carriage analog director. If the director failed to work in combat for whatever reason, the tracer element within the 37-mm ammunition would still provide some fire control direction for the gun crew.

With the introduction of a superior 40-mm antiaircraft gun into army service during World War II, the M1A2 37-mm antiaircraft gun took a secondary role, although it would continue to see some service until the end of the conflict.

40-mm Antiaircraft Gun

Even as the Ordnance Department continued to work out the bugs in its American-designed 37-mm antiaircraft gun, a far superior weapon of roughly the same size and capabilities appeared on the scene. That weapon was a 40-mm antiaircraft gun from the Swedish firm of Bofors. Developed with

The M15A1 Multiple Gun Motor Carriage consisted of two air-cooled M2 .50-caliber machine guns positioned on either side and slightly below an M1A1 37-mm antiaircraft gun. The rate of fire of the 37-mm gun was 120 rounds per minute. The top portion of the armor plates at the front of the gun mount could be lowered (as pictured) for better visibility and depression of the guns. There was no armor protection behind the gun mount, giving the crew more room to service the weapons with ammunition. *National Archives*

Crewmen of a U.S. Army 40-mm Bofors M1 antiaircraft gun prepare to fire on enemy aircraft. The gun is dug in next to a liberated section of the German Siegfried Line. All 40-mm ammunition for the Bofors consisted of fixed rounds, either armor piercing with tracer or high-explosive. The gun was traversed and elevated by manually operated controls. *National Archives*

the help of German engineers in the late 1920s, the Swedish gun, in the opinion of many military experts, was a much better weapon than the American 37-mm gun. The Swedish gun and carriage together weighed some 575 pounds less than the American gun and carriage. It fired a slightly larger (two-pound) and more powerful projectile at a higher muzzle velocity than its American counterpart. The Swedish gun also had a slightly faster rate of fire. If the barrel overheated from firing on the Swedish gun, it could be replaced in less than two minutes.

The higher rate of fire attained by the Swedish 40-mm antiaircraft gun was achieved with an automatic loading mechanism that fed cartridges into a loading tray from which they were pushed into the firing chamber by a mechanically operated rammer. Once fired, the spent case was ejected and the gun was ready for another round in a sequence that would continue as long as the gunner pressed the trigger and ammunition was being supplied.

So impressive was the Swedish-built 40-mm antiaircraft gun (more often simply called the Bofors) that by 1939 it was in widespread use throughout Europe. Frequently, the countries interested in acquiring the gun, including Great Britain and Germany, obtained the license rights to build it themselves.

The Bofors Company tried to interest the U.S. Army in buying its gun in 1937, but due to a misunderstanding regarding the purchase price of the weapon, nothing came of the deal. Instead, it fell to the U.S. Navy to interest the army in taking another look at the Swedish gun. This strange turn of events occurred when an American businessman with U.S. Navy connections saw the gun demonstrated in Sweden in 1939. He spoke so highly of what he saw that the navy decided to acquire an example for testing purposes in October 1940.

The navy invited the army to test the 40-mm antiaircraft to see whether they could standardize a single weapon for both services. The army took up the navy challenge and borrowed a British army version of the weapon mounted on a four-wheel trailer in December 1940. The army was so impressed with the gun it quickly sought out manufacturing rights from the Swedish company.

Chapter Five

Pictured in the street of a captured German city near the end of the war is a 40-mm Bofors antiaircraft gun M1. The posture of the gun crew suggests little threat from aerial attack. The gun and mount weighed in at 5,549 pounds. The 1.96-pound high-explosive shell left the barrel of the Bofors at a muzzle velocity of 2,870 feet per second. The maximum effective ceiling was 23,622 feet. *National Archives*

Even before contracts with the Swedish company could be formalized, the army officially adopted the British-built version of the Bofors gun in service as the 40-mm automatic antiaircraft gun M1 in April 1941. This was done with the understanding that as soon as quantity manufacture was achieved, the 40-mm gun was to replace the 37-mm antiaircraft gun already in army service. That moment was not reached until the summer of 1943. This delay was due to the time-consuming necessity of transposing the metric measurements of the foreign drawings to United States Ordnance standards, and the navy's higher priorities on the gun for its ships.

The U.S. Army felt very strongly that the mount and carriage of the British army version of the Swedish gun could be modified to better suit American-manufacturing methods. The Firestone Tire and Rubber Company, which accepted the contract for the first pilot models, succeeded in producing a welded frame to replace the riveted construction found on the British version. This modification in its design, plus a number of other important improvements, led to assigning the nomenclature M2 to the improved American-built carriage.

In an effort to improve the mobility of the 40-mm antiaircraft gun and increase its effectiveness, the Ordnance Department attempted to install the 40-mm antiaircraft gun and mount on the chassis of an M3 half-track. The weight of the gun and its supporting equipment badly overloaded the chassis of the M3 half-track and the project was eventually canceled.

In an effort to seek out a more suitable self-propelled chassis, the Army Ground Forces approved in May 1943 a request from the Antiaircraft Artillery Board to install a twin 40-mm antiaircraft gun mount on the modified open-topped and lengthened chassis of the T24 light tank. The vehicle was designated the Twin 40-mm Gun Motor Carriage M19 and was standardized after some minor changes in June 1944. Production began in April 1944 and none saw combat before the war ended.

Pictured on display is an M19 Motor Gun Carriage belonging to the Virginia Museum of Military Vehicles. The main armament of the M19 consisted of two 40-mm M2 Bofors antiaircraft guns in a twin mount. The gun mount could be traversed a full 360 degrees, and the guns elevated up to 90 degrees and depressed to minus 5 degrees. A crew of four men operated the guns. *Michael Green*

Appendix

Suggested Reading

Baily, Charles M. *Faint Praise: American Tanks and Tank Destroyers During World War II.* Hamden, CT: Achorn, 1983.

Canfield Bruce N. *U.S. Infantry Weapons of World War II.* Lincoln, RI: Andrew Mowbray Publishers, 1994.

Chamberlain, Peter, and Chris Ellis. *British and American Tanks of World War II.* New York: Arco, 1981.

Crouch, Howard R. *U.S. Small Arms of World War II.* Falls Church, VA: SCR Publications, 1984.

Constance McLaughlin Green, Harry C. Thompson and Peter C. Roots. *United States Army in World War II, The Technical Services, The Ordnance Department: Planning Munitions for War.* Office of the Chief of Military History, Department of the Army. Washington, D.C., 1953.

Forty, George. *United States Tanks of World War II.* Poole, Dorset, England: Brandford Press, 1983.

Gudgin, Peter. *Armoured Firepower: The Development of Tank Armament 1939-45.* Gloucestershire, England: Sutton Publishing Limited, 1997.

Hogg, Ian V. *Allied Artillery of World War II.* Marlborough, England: The Crowood Press Ltd., 1998.

Hogg, Ian V. *Allied Artillery of World War I.* Marlborough, England: The Crowood Press Ltd., 1998.

Hogg, Ian V. *The Illustrated Encyclopedia of Artillery.* Secaucus, New Jersey: Chartwell Books, 1988.

Hogg, Ian V. *The Encyclopedia of Infantry Weapons of World War II.* Greenwich, CT: Bison Books Corp, 1977.

Hogg, Ian V. *The Illustrated Encyclopedia of Ammunition.* London: New Burlington Books, 1988.

Hunnicutt, R. P. *Sherman: A History of the American Medium Tank.* Novato, CA: Presidio Press, 1978.

Hunnicutt, R. P. *Stuart: A History of the American Light Tank.* Novato, CA: Presidio Press, 1992.

Lida Mayo. *United States Army in World War II, The Technical Services, The Ordnance Department: On Beachhead and Battlefront.* Office of the Chief of Military History, Department of the Army. Washington, D.C., 1991.

Harry C. Thomson and Lida Mayo. *United States Army in World War II, The Technical Services, The Ordnance Department: Procurement and Supply.* Office the Chief of Military History, Department of the Army. Washington, D.C., 1960.

Perret, Geoffrey. *There's A War To Be Won; The United States Army in World War II.* New York, NY: Random House, 1991

Weeks, John. *Men Against Tanks, A History of Antitank Warfare.* New York: Mason/Charter, 1975.

Weeks, John. *Infantry Weapons.* New York, NY: Ballatine Books, Inc., 1971.

Index

601st Tank Destroyer Battalion, 123
704th Tank Destroyer Battalion, 115
Airborne Command, 39, 149
Allen, Major General Terry, 123
American Expeditionary Force (AEF), 107
Antiaircraft Artillery Board, 157
Army Air Corps, 33
Army Ground Forces (AGF), 10, 60–62, 65, 74, 101, 109, 111, 119, 123, 128, 157
Artillery Definitions, 42
Artillery Tactical Classifications, 43
Auto-Ordnance Corporation, 24, 26, 27
Baldwin, Hanson, 88
Bane, Major Paul A. Jr., 97
Battle of the Bulge, 65, 66, 111, 112, 123, 143, 150
Bayonets, 8, 9
Beretta, 24
Bergmann, 24
Bofors Company, 154, 155
Bradley, General Omar, 63, 74, 124
Bradley's First Army, 60, 63, 64
Brooks, Lt. Clinton, 129
Browning, John M., 9, 14, 29–31, 33, 34, 153
Bruce, Brigadier General Andrew D., 113, 118
Buck, Frank, 116
Burns, Bob, 36
Carbines, 21–24
Cavalry Board, 8
Cheney Bigelow Wire Works Company, 38
Chrysler Corporation, 78
Cleveland Tractor Company, 114
Coast Artillery Branch, 139
Coast Artillery Corps, 130, 133, 141, 149
Colt Patent Firearms Company, 9, 10, 30, 153
D-Day, 63, 111
Devers, Major General Jacob L., 112
E.G. Company, 38
Eisenhower, General Dwight, 38, 40, 96, 101, 128
Field Artillery Board, 47, 48
Firestone Tire and Rubber Company, 157
First Army, 124
First Cavalry Division, 8
First Infantry Division Museum, 72, 75
Ford Motor Company, 115
Forster, Sergeant Earnest B., 126
Fourth Armored Division, 90, 115
Garand, John C., 16, 18, 19
General Electric, 37, 38

Gillem, Major General Alvan C., 96
Green, Dr. Samuel G., 34
Handguns, 9–11
Heintz Manufacturing Company (Philadelphia), 148
Heintz Manufacturing Company design, 149
Hunnicutt, Dick, 61
Hyde, George J., 28
Infantry Board, 9
Infantry School, 131
International Business Machine (IBM), 16
Johnson, Melvin, 20
L.C. Smith & Corona Typewriter Company, 12
Lewis, Corporal Donald E., 39
Life magazine, 20
Lima Locomotive Works, 82
Lucas, Major General John L., 123
Lynch, Major General George A., 113
MacArthur, General Douglas, 19
Marine Corps, 20
Marine Corps, 26
Marlin Firearms Company, 28
Marlin-Rockwell Corporation, 15
Marshall, 112, 114
Marshall, Chief of Staff General George C., 109
Maxson Company, 150
McNair, Brigadier General Lesly J., 54, 62, 97, 109, 112–114
Miller, Corporal James A., 84
Moceri, Sergeant Nick, 97
Napolean, 41
National Rifle Association (NRA), 20
New England Small Arms Corporation, 16
New England Westinghouse Corporation, 30
New York Times, 88
Observations on the German Mark V Panther Tank, 98, 99
Ordnance Department, 6, 7, 9, 11, 12, 15, 16, 18–20, 24, 26, 28–31, 35–39, 46–49, 51, 52, 55, 56, 60, 62, 67, 76, 78, 85, 86, 91, 92, 94, 96, 97, 100–102, 104, 106, 110, 112, 114, 116, 117, 119, 122, 126, 128, 133, 141, 148–154, 157
Oyler, First Lieutenant Ural E., 95
Patton, 6, 16, 39, 40, 54, 57, 74, 77, 89–91, 95, 96, 102, 111, 112, 115, 123, 143, 152
Patton's Seventh Army, 68
Patton's Third Army, 46, 60, 63, 64, 65, 70, 88, 89, 90, 95, 101, 111
Pearl Harbor, 27, 45, 57
Perosa, Villar, 24

Pershing, General John J., 54
Porter, General, 69
Pressed Steel Car Company, 94, 95
Rathburn, Tank Commander Sergeant Harold S., 87
Remington Arms Company, 11, 12, 30
Rock Island Arsenal, 6, 11, 148
Roosevelt, President Franklin D., 85, 119, 151
Savage Arms Company, 26
Schaubel, First Lieutenant William, 97, 100
Schneider, 43, 60
Semiautomatic rifles, 16–21
Semmens, Colonel Paul E., 131
Signal Corps, 139
Skinner, Leslie A., 37
Smith & Wesson, 10
Spanish Civil War, 141
Springfield Armory, 6, 9, 11, 16, 19
Summerall, Charles P., 46
Tank Destroyer Force, 111, 112, 115, 118, 119, 122–124, 126, 128
The Hammer of Hell, 131
Third Army, 6, 40, 152
Thompson, John Taliaferro, 24
U.S. Army Desert Training Center, 146
U.S. Army Ordnance Department, 10, 72, 73
U.S. Army Ordnance Museum, 41
U.S. Army, 6, 8, 18, 19, 21, 27, 29, 33–36, 41–43, 46, 50, 51, 62, 67, 69, 70, 72, 74, 78–80, 87, 103–105, 107–109, 113, 115, 118, 128, 130–132, 134, 136–141, 143–145, 147–150, 152, 153, 155, 157
U.S. Army's Chemical Warfare Service (CWS), 67, 68
U.S. Army's First Infantry Division, 123
U.S. Marine Corps, 80
U.S. Navy, 26, 155
Virginia Museum of Military Vehicles, 74, 76, 78, 82, 115, 117, 127
War Department, 38, 106, 109, 112, 113, 141
Washington Post, 88
Westervelt Board, 43, 44, 47, 54, 56, 62
Westervelt, Brigadier General William I., 43
Winchester Repeating Arms Company, 15, 19, 21

Weapons
3-inch AA gun M1918, 133
3-inch antiaircraft gun, 117
3-inch GMC M10, 122
3-inch GMC, 120

3-inch gun carriage M1, 123
3-inch gun carriage M6, 123
3-inch gun M5, 123, 124, 126
3-inch M1917 Antiaircraft gun, 133–136
4.2-inch Mortar, 67–71
8-inch Gun M1, 64, 65
8-inch gun, 61–65
8-inch howitzer, 56–60
13-pounder(3-inch) Mark 3 antiaircraft gun, 131
25-pounder gun, 42
35-mm Antitank gun M3A1, 118
37-mm Antiaircraft gun, 151–154
37-mm Antitank gun M1A1, 119
37-mm cannon (Trench Gun), 104
37-mm gun M1916, 105
37-mm gun M1A2, 153
37-mm gun M2, 104
37-mm gun M3A1, 107, 112, 113, 120, 121
37-mm gun, 104
37-mm M6 gun, 115
37-mm Pak 36 antitank gun, 105
40-mm antiaircraft gun, 154–157
40-mm Bofors M1 antiaircraft gun, 155, 156
57-mm Antitank Gun M1, 110, 111
57-mm gun M1, 111, 112
60-mm M1 Mortar, 68, 69
60-mm Mortar, 66, 67
75-mm field gun, 106
75-mm gun M1987, 108, 109
75-mm howitzer, 77, 106
75-mm M1897A2, 113
75-mm Mle 1897 gun (French 75), 131
75-mm Pack howitzer M1, 44
75-mm Pack Howitzer M1A1, 107
76-mm antitank gun, 112
76-mm gun, 96, 97, 112, 127, 128
81-mm M1 Mortar, 68, 69
81-mm Mortars, 66, 67
90-mm antiaircraft batteries, 142
90-mm antiaircraft gun M1, 140–142, 145
90-mm antiaircraft gun, 126, 143–145, 153
90-mm antitank gun, 112
90-mm GMC M36, 127, 128
90-mm gun, 101, 128, 129
105-mm howitzer, 46, 126
155-mm Gun Motor Carriage M12, 58
155-mm gun, 56–60
155-mm howitzer, 54–56

159

155-mm Long Tom, 62
240-mm Howitzer M1, 61–63
240-mm Howitzer, 61–65
Aircraft warning devices, 136–141
Antiaircraft machine guns, 145–149
BAR, 14, 15, 30
Bazooka, 36–39
Brandt 81-mm mortar, 67
British Army Achilles, 125
Browning Automatic Rifle, 12, 13
Combination antiaircraft gun mounts, 151, 152
Elevator Cradle M1, 148
Enfield rifle, 35
Ford Motor T22 six-wheel armored car, 115
French 75 gun, 43, 47
French GPF 155-mm gun, 59
Fuses, 143
General Electric searchlight M1941, 137
GMC M10, 127
Grenade Launchers, 35, 36
Grenades 35, 36
Height-finding radar unit SCR-547, 143, 144
Howitzer, 42
Johnson semiautomatic rifle, 20
Long Tom gun, 57, 58, 60–62
M.G. (machine gun), 30
M1 bayonet, 9
M1 bazooka launcher, 38
M1 Carbine, 20, 23, 24, 36
M1 Garand semiautomatic rifle, 36
M1 grenade launcher, 36
M1 grenade, 35
M1 guns, 56, 57, 94, 115
M1 howitzer, 54, 55
M1 Mortar, 67
M1 Optical Height Finder, 142
M1 rifle, 15–21, 36
M1 rocket launcher, 38
M1 semiautomatic rifle, 26, 27
M10 GMC, 118, 124, 125
M10 Tank Destroyer, 124
M10 tank, 123
M10 vehicle, 119, 126
M10A1 medium tank, 118
M12 GMC, 60, 61
M13 armored half-tracks, 150
M13 Multiple gun motor carriage, 150
M13 two-gun, 151
M15 Combination Gun Motor Carriage, 151, 152
M15, grenade, 35
M15A1 Combination Gun Motor Carriage, 152
M15A1 multiple gun motor carriage, 154
M16 Multiple Gun Motor Carriage, 151, 152
M17 impact fragmentation grenade, 36
M18 GMC, 117
M18 gun motor carriage (GMC), 116, 115
M18 tank destroyer, 128
M18 vehicle, 119
M1897A2 75-mm field gun (French 75), 107
M1897A2 75-mm gun, 116
M19 Motor Gun Carriage, 157

M1903 rifle, 11, 12
M1903A3 rifle, 12
M1903A4 rifle, 12, 13
M1905 bayonet, 6–9
M191 machine gun, 31
M1911 automatic pistol, 9, 10
M1911A1 automatic pistol, 8–11
M1916, 104
M1917 155-mm gun, 61
M1917 artillery howitzer, 41, 43
M1917 gun, 42
M1917 howitzer, 53
M1917 light tank, 72
M1917 machine gun, 29–31
M1917 medium howitzer, 54
M1917A1 155-mm gun, 61
M1917A1 gun, 43
M1917A1 machine gun, 27–32
M1918 3-inch antiaircraft gun, 121
M1918 howitzer, 43, 53, 54
M1918A1 155-mm gun, 59, 61
M1918A1 rifle, 15
M1918A2 rifle, 14
M1918M1 gun, 43
M1919A4 machine gun, 30, 31
M1919A6 machine gun, 31, 32
M1921 "Tommy Gun," 26
M1921 submachine gun, 24
M1921, machine gun 33
M1921A1 machine gun, 31, 33
M1922 rifle, 15
M1928A1 "Thompson" submachine gun, 20–22
M1928A1 submachine gun, 26, 27
M1A1 37-mm antiaircraft gun, 153, 154
M1A1 90-mm antiaircraft gun, 143
M1A1 carbine, 24
M1A1 gun, 94, 142, 143
M1A1 height finder, 143
M1A1 howitzer, 44, 45
M1A1 Thompson submachine gun, 23
M1A1C gun, 94
M1A2 37-mm antiaircraft gun, 154
M1A2 gun, 94
M2 75-mm gun, 79
M2 90-mm antiaircraft gun, 144, 146
M2 antiaircraft gun, 133
M2 armored half-track, 112, 150
M2 grenade, 35
M2 gun, 78, 143
M2 half-track, 151
M2 HB machine gun, 85
M2 howitzer, 48
M2 machine gun, 33, 34, 146–148, 154
M2 Mortar, 70, 71
M2 submachine gun, 28
M20 fuse setter-shell rammer, 144
M21 armored half-track, 67
M24 light tank, 75, 76, 77
M26 Pershing heavy tank, 101, 129
M2A1 light tank, 72, 117
M2A1 medium tank, 76, 78
M2A3 light tank, 73
M2A4 light tank, 73, 74
M3 37-mm antitank gun, 106
M3 75-mm GMC, 117, 118
M3 75-mm gun, 83–85
M3 90-mm gun, 100, 101

M3 105-mm howitzer, 50
M3 antiaircraft gun, 133, 136
M3 armored half-track, 50
M3 GMC, 116, 119, 123
M3 half-track, 150, 151, 157
M3 howitzer, 48
M3 light tanks, 72–75
M3 medium tank, 60, 77–79, 120, 121
M3 submachine gun, 24, 25, 29
M3 tank gun, 106
M33 turret, 150
M36 battle tank, 129
M36 tank destroyer, 100, 101
M3A1 37-mm antitank gun, 110
M3A1 GMC, 116, 117
M3A1 light tank, 74
M3A1 medium tank, 79
M3A1 submachine gun, 29
M3A1, tank gun, 106
M3A3 light tank, 73, 74
M4 bayonet, 9
M4 medium tank (Sherman), 79–83
M4 Sherman, 85–87, 133
M40 155-mm GMC, 61
M40 Gun Motor Carriage, 59
M42 gun mount, 151, 152
M45 Mount, 150, 151
M4A1 Sherman medium tank, 118
M4A1 Sherman, 79, 81, 82, 86, 88, 90
M4A1 tank, 96
M4A1(76)W Sherman, 100
M4A1(76)W vehicle, 94, 95
M4A1, 80
M4A2 medium tank, 118
M4A2 Sherman, 79, 85
M4A3 medium tank, 51, 70
M4A3 Sherman, 79, 80, 86, 88, 90–92
M4A3 tank, 97
M4A3 vehicle, 94, 95
M4A3(76)W HVSS Sherman, 97
M4A3(76)W HVSS, 92, 93
M4A3(76)W Sherman, 96
M4A3E2 "Jumbo" assault tank, 95
M4A3E2 assault tank, 73
M4A3E2 Sherman, 89, 91
M4A3E8 Easy Eight tank, 95
M4A3E8 pilot vehicle, 92
M4A4 Sherman, 79
M4A6 Sherman, 79
M4E6 vehicle, 94
M5 Cletrac tank destroyer, 114
M5 light tanks, 72–75
M5 tank gun, 106
M51 carriage, 151
M54 mount, 152
M5A1 tank, 74, 75
M6 GMC, 119, 120
M6 rocket, 37, 38
M6 tank destroyer, 116
M6 tank gun, 106
M63 mount, 149
M6A1 rocket, 39
M7 3-inch gun, 188
M7 grenade launcher, 36
M7 Howitzer Motor Carriage, 49
M7 howitzer, 50, 51
M7A1 howitzer, 51

M7B1 machine gun, 50
M8 75-mm howitzer, 46
M8 armored car, 115
M8 grenade launcher, 36
M9A1 antitank rifle grenade, 36
M9A1 bazooka, 39
M9A1 rifle grenade, 36, 38
M9A1 rocket launcher, 39
Machine guns, 29–34
Mark II grenade, 35
Mark V heavy tank, 72
MI897A4, 107
Mle 1897 gun, 41
Mle 1917 artillery howitzer, 41
Model 1903 "Springfield," 11
Model 1917 double action revolver, 9, 10
Mortar Carrier M4, 66
Mortar M1, 66
Mortars, 65, 66
MP18 submachine gun, 24
Multiple Caliber .50 Machine Gun Mount M45, 150, 152
Multiple Caliber .50-Machine Gun Carriage M51, 150
Multiple Gun Motor Carriage M13, 150
Multiple Gun Motor Carriage M16, 150
Multiple machine gun mounts, 149–151
Pak (antitank) 36, 104
Pattern 1914 rifle, 13
Renault FT-17, 72
Rocket AT (Antitank) M1, 37
SCR-268, 140, 141
SCR-270 long-range, 140, 141
SCR-584, 140
Searchlight, 136, 137
Sound detection devices, 136–138
Springfield rifle, 20, 21, 35, 36
Stokes Mortar, 66, 67, 105
Submachine guns, 24–29
T-10 20-mm Oerlikon guns, 150
T19 Howitzer Motor Carriage, 49
T19 howitzer, 50
T2 carriage, 56
T24 light tank, 76, 77
T24 vehicle, 120
T26 heavy tank, 101
T28E1 Combination Gun Motor Carriage, 151
T34 Rocket Launcher, 70
T35 medium tank, 121, 122
T35E1, 122
T5 medium tank, 78
T5E2 gun, 78
T6 Gun Motor Carriage (GMC), 60
T6 medium tank, 80
T7 light tank, 76, 77
T71 destroyer weapon, 128
T71 pilot vehicle, 126
Thompson submachine gun, 24
Thompson submachine gun, 27, 28
Twin 40-mm gun motor carriage M19, 157
Twin Caliber .50 Machine gun, mount M33, 150
Vickers Mark VI 8-inch howitzer, 43
Vivien Bessler grenade, 35

160